Bruce Larson

Thirty Days to a New You

Edited by Hazel Larson

**ZONDERVAN
PUBLISHING HOUSE**   OF THE ZONDERVAN CORPORATION
GRAND RAPIDS, MICHIGAN 49506

ABOUT THE BOOK

This book is the creation of my wife, Hazel. It was her belief that a collection of contemporary parables might provoke a contemporary experiment of faith. She selected, compiled, and edited the parables from sermons and talks and from material previously published. I am grateful to the Zondervan Publishing House and Word, Incorporated for their graciousness in permitting us to use material from *Dare to Live Now, Living on the Growing Edge, Setting Men Free* (Zondervan), and from *No Longer Strangers* and *The One and Only You* (Word, Inc.).

Bruce Larson

Unless otherwise indicated, all Scripture is taken from *The New International Version,* copyright ©1973 by The New York Bible Society International and is used by permission.

30 DAYS TO A NEW YOU
Copyright ©1974 by The Zondervan Corporation
Grand Rapids, Michigan

Library of Congress Catalog Card Number: 74-4963

Printed in the United States of America.

CONTENTS

Part III / DOING THE WILL OF GOD

FOREWORD

This book comes out of my own years of experimenting with ways to discover God and know His will. It has been prepared with the hope that it will help many people make their own unique and significant discoveries about the nature of God and about their own potential.

This book is based on two profound convictions. First of all, I believe God is continually revealing Himself through His creation. He is doing this in the grand designs of history, but He also is revealing Himself, as in the days of old, in the ordinary, the trivial, and the commonplace.

The gospels report that Jesus spoke in parables. He simply looked around and saw the hand of His Father in everyday things. Jesus, who Himself is the greatest revelation of God, was able to communicate God's words to us through simple parables. He spoke of a coin lost, of a farmer planting a field, of a father with a wayward son, of a woman baking bread,

7

or of a man pressing grapes into wine.

And God is still communicating with His creatures in all of the common occurrences of our days. He is trying to say something about Himself and about us and about what life is meant to be if only we can see and understand.

The second conviction underlying this book is that few of us ever begin to be the person God meant us to be. Most of us have either settled for our present state or, at most, aspire to being a little better than we are with some more self-effort or education.

But the recurring message of the New Testament is that we can be so much more than we are. In fact, it promises that our spirits can be so linked with God, by the invasion of His Holy Spirit, that we begin to see with His eyes and love with His love and be a part of His creation and recreation.

This little book, then, is based on these two convictions: that God is revealing Himself daily in the commonplace and that, in Him, you can be more than you are — in fact, you can be *new.* I feel sure that anyone who will agree to read the book with the following stipulations can discover these for himself.

This book is *not* meant to be read at one sitting. It is a series of daily experiments. Simply read one of these each day for thirty consecutive days. Read it sometime in the morning, at the beginning of each day. Then apply the lesson during that day. Explore and experiment to see whether or not this particular insight is true for you. Notes should be kept about reactions and experiences. A blank page is provided for this after each daily exercise. By keeping this journal, you will begin to discover a God who is trying to communicate something fresh and exhilarating and exciting to you as a unique creation.

If you are now in a small group or want to start a study group or house-church, perhaps each member could covenant to do the same exercises individually and then report to each other when the group meets on all that each has been involved in as a result of these daily experiments.

Whether this experiment is conducted alone or as a group, I believe God has a great adventure for each one of us, and that adventure must begin where we are. It begins as we raise our own capacity for expectation — the expectation that God will begin to meet us as we look for Him in everyday occurrences. And in this great adventure, even though He begins where we are, He will not leave us as He finds us!

Part I

DISCOVERING
THAT I AM A CHILD OF GOD

The new you must find the true you, and the true you is reflected in the eyes of your Father who loves you just as you are.

1

Parable: The Letter

It seems I never lose my childlike sense of anticipation for what the daily mail might bring. Usually
it's bills or circulars or endless printed things. But on
the good days I find a letter from an old friend or
from one of our children away at school or a letter
of appreciation from someone who is reading one of
my books.

One of those welcome letters came recently from
a minister in Grand Rapids, Michigan. We had never
met, but it seems that while he was reading my
book, *Ask Me To Dance,* his seventeen-year-old son
was killed in an automobile accident. This new
friend went on to tell me how the book had been a
needed reminder for him and his wife of God's love
and resources in this time of grief. He also enclosed
a copy of a letter he had written to his son on the
day he was born which was to have been opened on
the boy's eighteenth birthday — the birthday he
would never celebrate.

The letter tells this new little boy of his parents' feelings as they anticipated his arrival and of their excitement about his birth. It goes on to talk of their hopes and dreams for his future and ends with these two wonderful paragraphs:

There are so many things that I should like to say to you today, bits of advice and words of suggestion for the life that awaits you. Suffice it all to say that you and your wonderful mother have made me the happiest man on earth. I have literally been walking on air!

...And now, you and I will be entering into a father-son relationship! Difficult sometimes, to say the least. I, too, had a father; and I know that I was a rascal on more than one occasion — and knowing that you will be a "chip off the old block," I predict the same for you. And on the other hand, sometimes I'll be a bit overbearing and somewhat of a problem to you; but do please bear with me. I know how wonderful your mother is — she'll be a referee deluxe and ever do her best to make our home always "home, sweet home." No matter what comes in the course of the years, might this passage from the parable of the prodigal son, where the father speaks to his elder son, ever govern and guide and guard that relationship between us. "My son, you and I are always together" (Luke 15:31). "Always together" in life and death, let us be.

I was deeply touched by this father's letter written seventeen years ago, and I wish that I had had the foresight to write such a letter to each of my own three children when they were born. But, beyond that, I believe a letter like this has been written to each one of us. Before you were a thought in your father's mind or a seed in your mother's womb, God knew your name and wrote you a letter.

In part He says, "John/Jane, there is nobody else like you. Nobody with your genes. Nobody with your past or potential experience. Nobody who will have your parents, your friends, or your influences. You are the only you that I made, and I want to tell you who you are and My dream for your future."

It is tragic that so many people never read the letter God wrote to them before they were born. They are like my new friend's son whose life ended before he could read the beautiful and moving letter of his father's dreams for him.

Word for the Day: John 1:47-48
"When Jesus saw Nathanael approaching, he said of him, 'Here is a true Israelite, in whom there is nothing false.'
'How do you know me?' Nathanael asked.
Jesus answered, 'I saw you while you were still under the fig tree before Philip called you.'"

Consciousness Raiser and Application

Have you ever felt misunderstood? There is a peculiar kind of loneliness that comes from feeling that no one really understands you.

One of the great serendipities in life is to meet a special person whom you instantly feel understands you and is on your wavelength. A kind of mystical relationship is established.

That must be exactly how Nathanael felt when he met Jesus for the first time. Nathanael was a genuinely good man. People like Nathanael who are without guile are often misunderstood by their peers and sometimes subject to ridicule. But in his meeting with Jesus, Nathanael experienced that moment we all long for — the moment of being both understood and appreciated.

Some of us, on the other hand, are very different from Nathanael. In overcoming a basic shyness, fear, or self-hate, we become loud or angry or negative people. But we also need the understanding of a friend who sees beyond all of the bluster, fuss, and anger to the scared child inside who longs to be known and understood.

Well, the good news of Jesus Christ is that God is our true parent and knows exactly who we are. He does not want our hopes and dreams to be shaped by the evaluations (negative or positive) of others. He knows that underneath all the negative defense mechanisms is a person unlike any other person who lives in hope that love can become a present reality and an abiding experience.

Today believe that God has written a letter addressed to you. It is unlike the letter He has written to anyone else. Don't meet the expectations of others, whether those expectations are "good" or "bad." Going to or from school or work or in be-tween chores at home, look for quiet times when you can listen to God. Let Him speak to you through the still small voice within or through the living parables being enacted all around you at the supermarket, gas station, or in a committee meeting. Believe that God wants to show you something of His dream for you today. Believe that you are known and loved. God's hope for you is that the unique person He created can begin to emerge and celebrate life.

Prayer
Oh Lord, create in me today an eagerness to read the letter written by You about me before I was born. Help me not to settle for the evaluations of others nor for their hopes for me nor even for my own self-evaluation. Make me eager to discover what Your hopes and dreams are for me. Help me to learn something about me that I have never known.

Journal (my reactions, insights, and results)

Parable: The Blue Ice

One of the joys of living in the Washington area is that you get to read the *Washington Post* every day. It is a newspaper full of all kinds of extraneous information. Recently an intriguing story appeared about a man who was working on his farm in Wisconsin when suddenly something dropped out of the sky into a field near him. It was blue, pock-marked, frozen, and mysterious.

Excitedly he chopped off a huge chunk, put it in his freezer, and called both the sheriff and some geologists from a nearby college to examine it. For a long time they were all stumped. Was it a meteor? Was it a piece of glacier carried by the jet stream? All they could deduce was that it was frozen hard and when it melted it smelled terrible! Finally someone solved the mystery. It turned out to be blue "potty fluid" accidentally ejected from an airplane toilet and frozen solid by the time it hit the ground.

You know, as I read that story I really identified

with that farmer. If I had had a mysterious gift drop out of heaven into my yard, I would have done just what he did — gather up as much of it as I could and preserve it in my freezer. And I suddenly realized how many things have dropped into my life and yours that are just like that. We feel compelled to preserve them or continue them because we assume they have been dropped from heaven and are therefore of value.

So many of our customs and traditions are in this category — sometimes even the life-style or vocation in which we find ourselves. A family business left by a generous father or a vocation chosen by a well-meaning mother can turn out to be smelly, frozen, and pock-marked and not God's gift for us at all. In the church we are often stuck with architecture, programs, committees, or methods that have apparently dropped on us from heaven via our great spiritual ancestors. How much we need to examine all those things we've been preserving, sort out the values and priorities in our freezers, and let some of them evaporate and disappear.

Word for the Day: Isaiah 43:18-19 (Revised Standard Version)
"Remember not the former things, nor consider the things of old. Behold, I am doing a new thing; now it springs forth, do you not perceive it?. . . "

Consciousness Raiser and Application

Think of all the things that make up your life: job, social life, commitments, community activities, family obligations.

Ask yourself these questions: Is this thing that I am involved in something I want to do? Does it give me enjoyment? Is it something that utilizes my gifts? Does it leave me exhilarated or debilitated? Is it of genuine help to other people? Do I believe in it thoroughly, and would I covet the same activity for others?

Find those things in your life that you are faithfully doing because they are inherited from members of your family or your church or society. Examine your job or the way you run your house, the courses you are taking in school, the committees on which you are now serving, your hobbies, your style of dress, your manner of talking, your way of looking at life, or God, or politics, or sex.

Today, whenever you have a free moment create some quiet spaces in your day and use them to think about your life and its components. Be aware that there may be some things at the center of your life that God would like to have you eliminate. Not necessarily because they are bad, but because they are not His best for you. Perhaps you heard God tell you to do something many years ago and you're still doing it because you are unable to hear Him saying to you today, "Enough. Stop." Remember Abraham was told to kill his son and then was given counter orders by the same God.

Are there things cluttering your life that are monotonous and dull and keeping you from fulfillment? If so, pray about them, discuss them with trusted friends, and then as an act of faith take steps to eliminate those things that are keeping you from finding the life-style God means you to have.

Prayer

Oh Lord, today give me security in the knowledge that I am loved irrevocably by You. Help me to sort through the contents in the freezer of my life that have come down to me from the past. May I save those which are of value to You in Your plan for my life and discard those good things which will simply impede what You have in mind for me.

Journal (my reactions, insights and results)

3

Parable: Mrs. K

When I was a student at Princeton Seminary, I spent weekends serving a church in a small town on the Hudson River — a church so small they couldn't afford a real preacher so they settled for me.

The vitality of that church was in the lay apostolate, the people who understood what it meant to be the people of God and who exercised this ministry. Mrs. K was one of those people.

Through all kinds of correspondence courses she had learned as much about the Bible as most preachers, and, more than that, if someone was in trouble Mrs. K heard about it and was there.

I've been away from that parish for over twenty years, but I visited Mrs. K in a nursing home recently, just before she died. There she was, in what I hope is a dying breed of nursing homes — an old converted house never meant for that purpose. I made my way up creaky stairs through bad odors and decaying people and finally found her. Still exercising her ministry to others, she had four or five friends gathered around to hear the opera on her little radio. Every Saturday afternoon she was hostess for the opera and could explain what was happening to her guests.

I said, "Hey. Mrs. K. It's your old preacher." Interrupting her party, she took me aside for a chat. Long a diabetes sufferer, she was now totally blind. When I asked how things were going, I discovered her husband had died and she was penniless and a welfare patient in the home, but she was radiant as she always had been.

"You know, Bruce," she said, "it's so wonderful here. If I don't feel like making my bed in the morning, they make it for me. All my meals are fixed for me, and if I ask them, they do my laundry. God is so good."

Remembering what a voracious reader she had always been, I had to ask, "Mrs. K, do you miss your sight?"

"Oh, yes," she said. "But you know, Bruce, I just remember all the wonderful things I've seen during my lifetime. Why, would you believe it, I went to the New York World's Fair *three* times!"

Mrs. K is gone now, but she's not gone. She is part of that great cloud of witnesses. With none of the externals of life that we think of as God's blessings, she still rejoiced and believed in Him.

That memorable visit with her reminded me of the scene from the play *The Unsinkable Molly Brown* where Molly sings "I Ain't Down Yet." And this ought to be the cry of God's people. To believe that God is with you in your present extremities. To say in your joy and sadness, "It isn't over. The last chapter isn't written. There is more, and I ain't down yet."

Word for the Day: Acts 7:54-58

> "When they heard this, they were furious and ground their teeth at him. But Stephen, filled with the Holy Spirit, looked up to heaven and saw the glory of God, and Jesus standing at the right hand of God. 'Look,' he said, 'I see heaven open and the Son of Man standing at the right hand of God.'
>
> At this they covered their ears and, yelling at the top of their voices, they all rushed at him, dragged him out of the city and began to stone him."

Consciousness Raiser and Application

What do you see when you are ringed about by enemies — enemies of old age or despair or death or failure or human enemies — all gnashing their teeth against you? Stephen saw the glory of God. Both the visible enemies and the invisible God are there. But it takes the gift of hope to see the invisible and be able to go down smiling.

Hope has little to do with facts, for there are always ample facts to cause one to be pessimistic, dour, and depressed. But there are just as many facts at hand to bring hope and expectancy, anticipation of marvelous things ahead. Nothing is hopeless — not the nation, your church, your family, or even your own life and future.

We do not greatly increase a person's ability to hope and dream simply by improving his condition. There are people who are surrounded by everything life has to give who are still cynical and sour. But the gift of hope is to be able to sort out and isolate all of the pluses in life, to build upon them, and to believe there are great days ahead.

Today ask God for the gift of hope and then apply that gift as you look around and within. Thank God for all the wonderful things that are already happening of which you are aware. This does not mean being a Pollyanna who thanks God for evil, but it means realizing that alongside the evil events perpetrated on us personally or taking place nationally there are also good and positive things that are just as indicative of the shape of the future. Look for them, believe them, and cultivate them. Begin to be a Mrs. K. Then wherever you are you will lift and encourage and bless people around you.

Prayer
Oh Lord, I am overly aware of all the slights and hurts and tragedies You have allowed to come to me at the hands of both my friends and strangers. Today make me aware instead of all the good things that have come and are coming and of all those gifts I possess. Stir in me the gift of joy and make me a giver of hope to others.

30 Days to a New You   27

Journal (my reactions, insights and results)

4

Parable: The Rock Concert

One snowy night several years ago, through some rather unusual circumstances, I found myself at the Fillmore East Theater in New York City, then the rock music capital of the world. My seventeen-year-old son and his friend were at a concert there and had discovered they would be too late to catch the last train back to New Jersey and home. A midnight phone call summoned me from my bed and sent me into New York by car to meet them at the theater during the last performance.

The Fillmore is gone now, but for many years it was, perhaps, the center of the whole rock culture in our land and the last place you would expect to find a middle-aged clergyman and suburbanite like me. Before I located those two boys, I wandered around for two hours, from 1:00 to 3:00 A.M., surrounded by three thousand hippies from fourteen to thirty.

Now in my mind, hippies all kind of looked alike — a long-haired, raggedy bunch. But in those two hours I learned how wrong I had been. Instead, their appearance seemed to be communicating: "There is nobody else in the world like me." One of them was dressed like Kit Carson with saddle bags and buckskins; one was wearing an 1890 Polish officer's coat; one girl wore a granny outfit; and another was dressed like a vamp of the thirties. There were three thousand different, wild costumes in the place and three thousand different hair styles. Their primary message seemed to be, "Don't confuse me with anybody else. I'm me."

Now when I was a teenager, which my children assume was before the Civil War, girls all wore bobby-socks and saddle shoes, and guys had to conform and be like the "in" group. As we became middle-aged we conformed again — first to gray flannel suits and eventually to something more mod.

Even we Christians tend to have a kind of religious conformity. But the uniqueness of the Christian message is that Jesus came to liberate us from conformity. And the miracle of the Body of Christ is that we find togetherness when we affirm our uniqueness. I don't know of any other organization in the world, political, religious, social, or fraternal, that does this.

Like the kids at the Fillmore East Theater, we can affirm our uniqueness and say to the world, "I'm me, and I want you to be you!"

Word for the Day: Matthew 5:48

> "Be perfect, therefore, as your heavenly Father is perfect."

Consciousness Raiser and Application

Our word for the day has given a great many people a great deal of trouble for a great many years. If it really means for us to be perfect as God is perfect, then we would all look just like Him and just like each other. But the word perfect in the original Greek really means "the perfect you." And if we are each admonished to be "the perfect you" God meant us to be, we begin to understand that creation is a place where God delights in lavish uniqueness. Billions and billions of snowflakes fall in every storm and no two are alike, and so our human perfection consists not of being like anyone else, but of discovering our uniqueness and being that to the glory of God.

For today, try to find the things that you can do or say or even wear to express your uniqueness. Many of us wear clothes which communicate that we are like all of the other people in our particular economic, social, and age group. We tend to talk like people who belong to our church or group. Today try to find ways of dressing and expressing yourself that act out your own uniqueness.

Send a signal that you are different and that you enjoy being different. If you plan to have lunch in a restaurant, even so small an act as having some new or strange dish can declare that you are not a conformist.

In the same way, be especially aware of the people around you today. They are sending out clues to their own uniqueness by what they are wearing or saying or doing. Affirm their attempt to be unlike anyone else by saying something about it and asking them what it really means. In each relationship you have today, one snowflake is meeting another. With all our myriad differences, we are one in our uniqueness. Celebrate that gift today.

Prayer
Oh Lord, it is impossible to comprehend the endless varieties of Your creation. Give me the eyes of faith to behold people I meet today as unrepeatable miracles. Increase my awareness of my own uniqueness as well as the uniqueness of every other person and help me celebrate those differences.

Journal (my reactions, insights and results)

5

Parable: Jock

I am a great dog lover, and our family has had a long succession of dogs over the years. While we were in a pastorate in Illinois, we had a beagle hound by the name of Jock. He was a miserable dog who destroyed my wife's rugs and the neighbors' shrubs and the nocturnal peace of the neighborhood. But he had one outstanding quality. He loved me deeply.

As I went to the church or the hospital or made pastoral calls, Jock used to follow my car and always arrived shortly after I did, much out of breath. When I saw him coming, I would always sternly rebuke him, but I was secretly pleased by his enthusiastic and total devotion.

Observing all this, my wife kept saying a prophetic word, as wives have a way of doing. She pointed out that if Jock wasn't chained or trained to stay at home he would surely be run over some day. Some day came. He was not only run over and killed — but by my own car. He caught up to me at a stop sign, and not knowing he was there, I ran over him.

There is certainly truth in the old song, "You Always Hurt the One You Love." But it wasn't my love for Jock that destroyed him. It was my great need for his love. It is this need for love that makes us destroy the very people for whom we care the most.

Word for the Day: Luke 15:11-13

> . . . "There was a man who had two sons. The younger one said to his father, 'Father, give me my share of the estate.' So he divided his property between them.
> Not long after that, the younger son got together all he had, set off for a distant country and there squandered his wealth in wild living."

Consciousness Raiser and Application

The miracle of God's love for us might be summed up in two words: sacrifice and freedom. At the heart of God's love is the sacrifice of His own Son, Jesus Christ, for us. Greater love hath no man than this. But God's love also allows us the freedom to make choices.

Our word for the day is from a parable about the nature of the love of God. A son is free to take his inheritance and squander it, not just foolishly, but harmfully. The father stands by and allows it all to happen. Indeed, he makes it possible by dividing the inheritance.

Your assignment today is to examine the primary relationships in your life — those relationships with the people you love the most. Are there some places where you are acting not out of someone else's best interests, but out of your need for them and their love? So many times we think we are acting out of love when we are really acting out of self-interest. We give advice not because the advice is needed, but because we have a need to control or be important. We do things for people we love not because they need what we're doing, but because we have a need to build ourselves into their way of life. Today, examine the visits or telephone calls you make and the letters you write. Do you reach out in communication because someone else has a need or because you have the need to be important to them?

Today ask God to give you a measure of His Spirit in your love for those nearest and dearest to you, friends or family. Try to see them through His eyes and let Him make you aware of their deepest needs. See if you can fill a need they have rather than a need you have. For twenty-four hours try to practice this kind of love in your most intimate relationships without telling anyone about it. See if you or they can tell the difference.

Prayer

Lord, You know what a self-centered and needy person I am. You know how much I parade my own unfulfilled needs and dishonest motives behind the mask of love. Today help me to be aware of the ways in which I try to manipulate those around me in the guise of love. Help me to love with the sacrifice and freedom that is Yours and that You will share with me if I ask. Help me to be an instrument for freeing those for whom I care the most.

Journal (my reactions, insights and results)

6

Parable: The Ashes

My father died when I was seventeen. I was in the army, and by the time I received word of his illness and traveled home, he was already dead. Perhaps because of these circumstances I had great difficulty in coming to grips with the fact of his death and carried a deep grief inside for a long time.

My father was cremated, and mother kept his ashes around for many years. Long after Hazel and I had established our home, mother married a wonderful man. In time my stepfather was able to suggest that he didn't want to live in a house with a former husband's remains, so mother gave my father's ashes to me. I was living then in Binghamton, New York, and I recall vividly the day I walked out alone in one of our beautiful state parks to a snowy hillside overlooking a lake — a place my father would have loved. I prayed and thanked God for him — who he was and what he had meant to me. Then I opened the box and threw his ashes to the wind.

Somehow in that act I "let go of my father," and the scattering of the ashes was to me sacramental and liberating. I am left with the memory of those seventeen years we shared together.

Word for the Day: 2 Timothy 1:3-7

> "I thank God, whom I serve, as my forefathers did, with a clear conscience, as night and day I constantly remember you in my prayers. Recalling your tears, I long to see you, so that I may be filled with joy. I have been reminded of your sincere faith, which first lived in your grandmother Lois and in your mother Eunice, and I am persuaded, now lives in you also. For this reason I remind you to fan into flame the gift of God, which is in you through the laying on of my hands. For God did not give us a spirit of timidity, but a spirit of power, of love and of self-discipline."

Consciousness Raiser and Application

For decades, depth psychologists have been telling us there is dynamite in our past. How you feel about your past and what you do with your past will determine to a large extent the kind of person you are today.

But beyond the psychological implications, Paul, in our word for the day, seems to be linking the past with authentic Christian living in the present. First of all, Paul claims that he served God as did his forefathers. He then reminds Timothy, his disciple and spiritual son, that the faith he has found began in his mother Eunice and his grandmother Lois. Finally he ties Timothy's heritage into an exhortation to live in power and love and self-discipline.

It seems to me there are two ways that the past can block authentic living in the present. First, I can forget the past and ignore it. I can believe that I dangle all alone in my present relationship to God. Well, this is not possible. Even if I have no spiritual inheritance from parents or grandparents, I still have spiritual ancestors who go all the way back to Pente-cost when Christ's church was born. Our spiritual heritage is enriching, and we need to claim it and thank God for it.

But it is also possible to so glory in the past that we cease to live in the present. Even Paul speaks about trading his tremendous heritage for the present riches of knowing Christ, and this is a paradox. We ought to enjoy the past but not let those glorious memories block us from the riches that God would give us now.

Abraham, the father of the faithful, made that incredible geographical and spiritual journey to the Promised Land with his beloved wife Sarah and a whole retinue of family, servants, and possessions. When at the end of the journey Sarah died,

Abraham's words were the words of a man of faith, "Give me property among you for a burying place that I may bury my dead out of sight." He knew that however much he had loved Sarah and would always love her, the dead must be buried and authentic living must continue.

Today remember some of the heritage that has come to you either from physical parents or from your spiritual ancestors. Read the eleventh chapter of Hebrews and know that you are a descendant of all the men and women mentioned there. If you have a particular friend or relative who has died and for whom you continue to grieve, in faith bury that person out of sight. Let them go, grateful for their influence and their love and in the certainty that you will meet again. Move on unafraid into tomorrow.

Prayer
Lord, I am a unique being partly because of my inheritance from the past. As I remember relatives, friends, teachers, and companions of the way who are a part of my past, help me to see them as a special gift and a personal treasure. But, Lord, at the same time let me bury that which is gone. Free me to live in the now with my eyes on the future. Fill me with Your Spirit — a Spirit of power, of love, and of self-discipline. I ask this for Your sake and for Your Kingdom.

Journal (my reactions, insights and results)

Parable: Two Tuxedos

Though I am in middle years, soon to approach senior citizenry, I find I am still haunted by thirty-five-year-old dreams of inadequacy and lack of preparation. Sometimes I am caught in situations that stir up these childhood memories.

Recently I was asked by an old army buddy to come down to his town in Virginia to speak to the annual dinner for the chamber of commerce. It was not until I was introduced at the banquet by my friend that I became aware of the fact that I was the only man in the dining room not wearing a tuxedo. All my past fears of inadequacy had to be conquered before I could go on with the speech I had prepared. You might not have known it to look at me, but at that moment I had become the small boy from the Great Depression in a hand-me-down suit, and it was unnerving.

Three months later I spoke at another chamber of commerce dinner at which I suffered a somewhat different kind of trauma. An old friend in upstate New York was being honored as the retiring president, and he had asked if I would be the speaker at the event. He informed me that it was a formal affair and added that he hoped I would not pull my usual cheapskate act and wear a clerical collar. So, determined to be prepared this time, I called the local tuxedo rental in our town, gave them my appropriate measurements, and arranged to pick up my finery the morning of my flight. When I went down to pick it up, I discovered that the only tuxedos rented in the swinging new town of Columbia were "mod" affairs with belted backs and purple lapels and the shirts amply decorated with lace. It was too late to do anything about it, so I gathered it all up and headed for the airport. That night before the chamber of commerce in Binghamton, New York, where literally hundreds of people were attired in the traditional "waiter's suit," I was resplendent in my Edwardian tux and ruffles. To make matters worse, it was the first time they had ever asked a clergyman to speak. "Some way for a spiritual type to appear at a secular banquet!" I thought. And again I had to fight down all the old fears from the past about wearing the wrong thing to the party. You know, if you're equally anxious about being overdressed or underdressed, it's hard to win.

Word for the Day: Mark 10:46-52

"Then they came to Jericho. As Jesus and his disciples, together with a large crowd, were leaving the city, a blind man, Bartimaeus (that is, the Son of Timaeus), was sitting by the roadside begging. When he heard that it was Jesus of Nazareth, he began to shout, 'Jesus, Son of David, have mercy on me!'

Many rebuked him and told him to be quiet, but he shouted all the more, 'Son of David, have mercy on me!'

Jesus stopped and said, 'Call him.'

So they called to the blind man, 'Cheer up! On your feet! He's calling you.' Throwing his cloak aside, he jumped to his feet and came to Jesus.

'What do you want me to do for you?' Jesus asked him.

The blind man said, 'Rabbi, I want to see.'

'Go,' said Jesus, 'your faith has healed you.'

Immediately he received his sight and followed Jesus along the road."

Consciousness Raiser and Application

I am convinced that spontaneity is one of the marks of a Christian faith. There is a lack of self-consciousness about a person of faith. There is no concern about being overdressed or underdressed, being "proper" or knowing "the right words."

In our word for the day, blind Bartimaeus knew that a great teacher was coming by who was reported to have the gift of healing. Poor Bartimaeus sat by the wayside, wanting more than anything else to see. Sensing that Jesus was passing by, he leaped up and said, "Look at me. I'm over here. Help me." Immediately people around him tried to hush him up. They were more concerned with being proper than they were with Bartimaeus's sight. But like a small child, he would not be silenced. He knew his one chance for healing was at hand, and he was willing to risk outraging his townsmen's sense of decorum. The beautiful part of the story is that Jesus responded to that spontaneous, unsophisticated cry and gave this man the gift of sight.

Faith is a childlike quality. If you offer a hungry child a meal or a thirsty child a drink, there is an immediate and spontaneous response. Offered a Good Humor bar or an ice cream cone, the child does not make a studied response, using just the right words.

So to live by faith means that you and I will grow less and less self-conscious. We will worry less about being properly dressed for each occasion. We will worry less about what "they" will say and think about us. In point of fact, "they" probably seldom think of us. Nevertheless, we're often paralyzed by fear of what they might be thinking. And we know that perfect love casts out fear.

Faith grows as we exercise it. Today, instead of living according to the rules prescribed by your social culture, try to do something spontaneous. Try to break with routine. This could mean befriending the checker at the supermarket or bringing some flowers home to your wife or mother. To be the person God meant you to be might mean breaking one or more of the shackles that your culture and your society have laid upon you. Look for ways to celebrate the new spontaneous you. Believe with Bartimaeus that Jesus has a gift to give you if you will break with convention and ask for it.

Prayer

Oh Lord, let me believe today that you have a gift for me. May my ingrown eyeballs, that always look within wondering how I'm doing and how others perceive me, not block that gift. May this be a day of spontaneous action rather than routine reaction. Let me open my eyes and see You and receive that which You would give me out of Your great love.

Journal (my reactions, insights and results)

Parable: The Watch

Many years ago I heard a story that made a deep impression on me. It concerned Henry B. Wright, a professor at Yale University and author of that classic *The Will of God and Man's Life Work.*

He was a man with a great concern for the well-being of friends, neighbors, and even strangers. Hearing that an old classmate had become an alcoholic living in the Bowery section of New York, he made a journey from New Haven one weekend to visit him. The visit seemed to accomplish nothing, however, and the return trip on the train found Wright in prayer for his friend.

During those prayers, God seemed to be giving him specific instructions: to buy a gold watch, have it inscribed, and send it to his friend. Knowing that God often spoke in strange ways, he obeyed. It seems the interest and concern expressed by that gift made such an impact on his friend that he stopped drinking immediately and returned to a useful life.

When the professor saw the effect of his gift, he decided to send the same kind of gold watch with the same inscription to another alcoholic friend. To Wright's chagrin, this man promptly sold the watch to buy liquor. It was a telling demonstration for Henry Wright and for us of the uniqueness of God's guidance.

Word for the Day: Acts 9:10-15

"In Damascus there was a disciple named Ananias. The Lord called to him in a vision, 'Ananias!'

'Yes, Lord,' he answered.

The Lord told him, 'Go to the house of Judas on Straight Street and ask for a man from Tarsus named Saul, for he is praying. In a vision he has seen a man named Ananias come and place his hands on him to restore his sight.' 'Lord,' Ananias answered, 'I have heard many reports about this man and all the harm he has done to your saints in Jerusalem. And he has come here with authority from the chief priests to arrest all who call on your name.'

But the Lord said to Ananias,
'Go! This man is my chosen instrument to carry my name before
the Gentiles and their kings and
before the people of Israel.'"

Consciousness Raiser and Application

The secret to spiritual effectiveness is being able
to cooperate with God's Holy Spirit. This simply
means being able to perceive God's will and to do it.

In our word for the day nothing could have seemed
more ridiculous to Ananias than to walk up to Judas's
house on Straight Street and ask to see the chief
enemy of every Christian in the land. After arguing
with God, Ananias had the grace to trust Him and
go, and that was the beginning of the great missionary
tale of all time. For Saul became the Apostle Paul,
God's link with the Gentiles.

God's Kingdom will not come through frantic
effort or even great zeal. You and I as believers can
try to promote it by knocking on every door in our
neighborhood or by buying full-page ads in the paper
or time on TV. This is not necessarily bad, but it is
not maximum.

God alone knows when people are ready for the
help He can give. Therefore, it is imperative that you
and I live our life daily in such a way that God can
break into our routine and prompt us to initiate a
phone call, a letter, a visit, or a conversation.

For me, there are two great blocks to living in this
sensitive and effective way. In the first place, I don't

really expect God to speak to me and so I allow little time for listening. Now God may give us a nudge in the middle of a frantic schedule, but it is also important to take time to be quiet during the day and allow God to give us specific guidance.

But the second problem I face is that after God has guided me in one particular situation, I then expect Him to work in that same way every time. Ananias could have made the mistake of going to Judas's house periodically for the rest of his life looking for someone else like Saul. But we can never generalize on the basis of past guidance. We must let God give us His fresh instructions for the present moment. Today, be dependent upon God and His Spirit for guidance. Take time to be quiet. Believe that some of the specific promptings you feel could be God's commands. Expect something fresh from God that will make you a partner with Him in sharing good news and bringing hope and healing in His Spirit.

Prayer

Lord, help me to believe You are more eager to guide me today than I am to receive Your guidance. Out of Your love, Lord, be patiently insistent with me until I begin to believe that You want to reveal Your will in my life. Help me to act on whatever guidance I receive in spite of my fears or my doubts. May I do this out of simple trust in You. Let me not be overly focused on results, but on Your word and on my own obedience.

Journal (my reactions, insights and results)

Parable: The Sailboat

Bermuda is one of my favorite places in the world. When some dear friends offered us their home there for a week in exchange for babysitting two Labrador retrievers, I got immediate guidance to go.

Part of the fun of Bermuda is zipping along on a motor bike on "the wrong side" of their narrow and curvy roads. One especially bright day my wife Haz and I went off on our two bikes for a day's excursion to the other end of the island.

We arrived at the old harbor in St. George's just in time to see an unusual sight. Five or six grizzled fishermen were gathered around the wharf watching a young man shove off in an old double-ender sailboat about twenty feet long. "You know where that crazy buzzard is going?" one man volunteered. "He's sailing to England." And as the little boat pulled out from the harbor, those veteran sailors only shook their heads in disbelief.

Somehow the sight of that one frail craft with its

lone crew stirred something deep inside me and, without meaning to, I found myself waving and shouting, "Bon Voyage." Surprised and obviously encouraged, the young captain waved back and continued to do so until his little boat was gone from sight.

For that young man getting there wasn't a certainty. He might not make it. But he had to start out. That's what life is all about. As Christians, whether we arrive or not isn't the issue. It's okay to fail as long as we launch out. Don't stay in the harbor.

Word for the Day: Acts 20:22-24

> "And now, compelled by the Spirit, I am going to Jerusalem, not knowing what will happen to me there. I only know that in every city the Holy Spirit warns me that prison and hardships are facing me. However, I consider my life worth nothing to me, if only I may finish the race and complete the task the Lord Jesus has given me . . . ."

Consciousness Raiser and Application

The Apostle Paul felt compelled to go to Jerusalem. He knew this was God's mandate for him and that he must comply.

It is not hard to understand the feelings of his companions. Those early Christians were aware that his life would be in danger in Jerusalem. They pleaded with him not to go into what seemed almost certain death.

But Paul knew that life in Christ is a life of both safety and security. God offers us the security of a home eternal in the heavens. We can be secure in the knowledge that our name is written in the Lamb's Book of Life; we are forgiven. We are loved. Nothing can ever separate us from the love of God in Jesus Christ.

But our security in God does not guarantee that we will be safe or untroubled or undamaged in this life. Paul knew there was more at stake than the length of his life or his physical safety. Paul knew he did not have to find safety nor even survive the journey. What he did know was that he must obey the guidance to launch out and to risk.

Today look for the place where you can trust Christ and begin to risk. It may mean believing that the Holy Spirit wants you to leave your present job and look for a new one. It may mean changing your major in school. It may mean risking a friendship by telling someone a vital truth about yourself. It may mean apologizing and saying you were wrong. It may mean risking your reputation on a great cause or your money in something that could fail.

But bear in mind: the important thing is not the success of the venture, but that you do what God is asking of you. You don't have to succeed, but you do have to try.

30 Days to a New You   *57*

Prayer
Oh Lord, as an act of faith this day, help me to cut the moorings and hoist the sail on some project that seems to have in it Your call for me and my life, whatever its chances for success.

Journal (my reactions, insights and results)

PART II

BECOMING A PART
OF THE FAMILY OF GOD

The new you belongs to a family not of your own choosing. Let God show you your new family and help you to find fresh ways to communicate with them.

10

Parable: Two Churches

It all began at a metropolitan airport where my plane was met by a young clergyman who had been assigned by his bishop to drive me to a meeting sponsored by their diocese. I had never met my chauffeur before, so as we drove along I asked him what kind of church he had. His answer was instant and electric. "I have a terrible church. I've had it for eight years, and I keep asking my bishop to move me but he never does. I can't stand it anymore."

"What's wrong with it?" I asked.

"My church is full of Archie Bunkers," he responded. "Have you ever watched 'All in the Family?'" I replied that it was my favorite TV program. "Then you'll know what I mean. I've got a blue-collar congregation full of cautious, bigoted people who equate God with the military-industrial complex." For the next half-hour my new friend delivered one of the strongest sermons against the silent majority I've ever heard.

Several months later an old friend who had taken a new church dropped in to see me. When I asked about the church, Howard immediately replied, "It's an exciting church. I can't wait to see what God is going to do with it." Describing his congregation enthusiastically he said, "It's a church full of Archie Bunkers. I've never known much about this segment of America before, but I find that there is pure gold beneath their many defense mechanisms. They really are the core of America's greatness. They have tremendous courage; they work hard; they are faithful, loyal people."

Now I don't have to be very wise and prophetic to guess which of these two churches will thrive and experience renewal and which will decline in faith and enthusiasm. What will make the difference? Basically these two congregations seem the same: filled with cautious, bigoted, reactionary people. But one pastor brings to the situation the gift of hope. He sees invisible qualities in his congregation, and with his vision of hope he will be able to call forth the real Archie Bunker, the Archie Bunker that the other pastor is unable to see.

My guess is that the second pastor will live in discouragement until his bishop finally moves him. And unless he receives the gift of hope somewhere along the way, he will always be the pastor of "a terrible church."

Word for the Day: Luke 19:1-7
"Jesus entered Jericho and was

passing through. A man was there by the name of Zacchaeus; he was a chief tax collector and was wealthy. He wanted to see who Jesus was, but being a short man he could not, because of the crowd. So he ran ahead and climbed a sycamore-fig tree to see him, since Jesus was coming that way.

When Jesus reached the spot, he looked up and said to him, 'Zacchaeus, come down immediately. I must stay at your house today.' So he came down at once and welcomed him gladly.

All the people saw this and began to mutter, 'He has gone to be the guest of a sinner.'"

Consciousness Raiser and Application

An important part of faith is the ability to see the unseen. Faith begins when we see the unseen God who reveals Himself in so many invisible yet tangible ways. But another dimension of faith is to begin to see the invisible in the life of people and groups all around us.

Everybody is partly dull, unimaginative, and re-actionary. But in the same way everybody has the potential to take his heritage, background, and gifts and become an exciting, creative member of society.

Potentially, everybody is a part of the household of faith.

Zacchaeus was an unlikely candidate for discipleship when Jesus summoned him down from his tree. A hated and dishonest tax collector, he could not in his wildest imaginings have guessed that the great teacher coming to his town would be staying at his house that day.

Look for those people around you about whom society has said, "They are hopeless." Your job today is to ask God for the eyes of faith. Look at that child who is failing; that colleague who is uncreative; that member of your committee or board who is overly cautious; that person who is opposed to you politically. Be aware of their potential and call it forth by a new attitude on your part.

You may not have a chance to say or do anything specific, but by simply beginning to appreciate that person — to see what he already is in part and what can emerge as his true personhood is discovered — you can work a miracle.

Today become a liberator of those Archie Bunkers who surround you. Pick one hopeless case, a person who has been confined by you to eddys of uncreativity or reactionary conservatism, whom you've been thinking of as a person with no potential. Make that person an object of your love, your prayers, and your dreams.

Prayer
Oh Lord, even as you called Zacchaeus down from

his tree and gave him a new life, help me today by all that I say and am to call forth in someone a new liberated individual who can celebrate life and bless his brothers.

Journal (my reactions, insights and results)

11

Parable: The Tie Clasp

Some years ago a friend of mine sent me an unusual tie clasp which I wear most of the time: two tiny crossed keys. Just after receiving it, I was flying with a friend on a short flight from Pittsburgh to Dayton. The plane was nearly empty, and as we moved to the rear to take our seats, one of the stewardesses caught sight of my tie clasp and exclaimed, "You're wearing keys!"

"Yes," I said.

"They are papal keys," she added.

I had not thought of that, but wanting to encourage her interest, I replied, "Yes, they are."

"What do they mean?" she asked rather suspiciously.

"Well," I said, "I believe that every Christian holds in his hands the keys to the Kingdom of God. Jesus said that those whom we let in come in, and those whom we keep out by our words or attitudes or relationships stay out."

Instantly the stewardess's face lit up. "I believe that too," she said. "I'm an underground Catholic. My friend over here, the other 'stew,' is an underground Methodist."

You can imagine how my friend and I responded to this news. No sooner was the plane aloft and the other passengers settled than the two girls came back and the four of us had a "small group meeting" all the way to Dayton.

We soon discovered that the stewardesses, who lived in San Francisco, were looking for some lively church contacts there. We suggested some names and then went on to share with them news of vital Christians like themselves in places like Dayton and New York, as well as San Francisco.

Later in thinking over this encounter, I began to wonder what would have happened if I had been wearing a more traditional symbol, such as a cross in my lapel. Or if I had been carrying a Bible in my hand. Perhaps these might have elicited the same response, but I'm not sure.

What do we mean to say when we wear a cross or carry a Bible? Is it: "Look, I am one with you. I am your friend. Trust me; count on me"? Or is it: "See my symbol? Now you know where I stand, so you'd better watch what you say and do!"

There is a creative kind of communication that we can discover as we live out our faith in the world. Those of us who choose to wear an identifying symbol should make sure it is not something just to make us feel secure, something to hide behind.

Rather, it should be a vehicle for initiating con-
versations, responses, and relationships.

Word for the Day: Mark 1:16-17

> "As Jesus walked beside the Sea
> of Galilee, he saw Simon and his
> brother Andrew casting a net into
> the lake, for they were fishermen.
> 'Come, follow me,' Jesus said,
> 'and I will make you fishers
> of men.'"

Consciousness Raiser and Application

The Lord has called you to be a fisher of men,
and someone has said that this is big game hunting.
Apparently it is not enough for us to simply pray
for people and ask God to reach them. We are more
than intercessors. We are called to be those who
actually go out and catch people for Jesus and His
Kingdom. This is what the priesthood of believers
is all about. We are those who become the means
by which Jesus reaches people, gets their attention,
and wins their allegiance. We are the priests who
are to love and support and affirm them as well as
hear their confession.

I think it is significant that the first time Jesus
used the term 'fishers of men' He was speaking to
fishermen, and they understood perfectly what He
meant. They understood the strategy that a fisherman uses in catching fish. If he uses a hook and a
line, then he needs something to attract the fish.
Either he baits the hook with something they like to

eat or he baits it with something that will attract their attention and which looks like something to eat. If the fisherman is using nets, then he must be careful not to scare the fish.

Jesus seems to be suggesting that fishing for men is a similar science. Our parable today indicates the need to be aware of the signs and the signals we give out to people, both by words and deeds. We need to intrigue people with the reality of God, the love that Jesus has for them, and the benefits that will result if they respond to Him.

So today your assignment is to become aware of the signals you are sending. How do other people read you, perceive you, understand you? Think of the last time you said to someone, "But that's not what I meant." Perhaps to your spouse in an argument, to one of your children, to your employer or employee, or to a friend. The other person may perceive something quite different than what you meant or said. So today become aware of how you come across to the other person: your words, the things you do, the gestures you make. Try to communicate verbally and non-verbally to people around you the fact that they are of worth, that God loves them just as they are, that life can be radically different. Try to speak and live and dress like someone who is literally bait for Christ and His Kingdom.

Prayer
Oh Lord, at the center of Your call to all men is a love so incredible, so amazing that it is almost beyond

belief. Today, help me to speak and live and dress and act so that Your incredible love can become more credible. Help me, in fact, to become the link by which another can accept and receive You and be caught by Your love.

Journal (my reactions, insights and results)

Parable: The Subway

During the many years that my office was located in New York City, I had the questionable pleasure of being a subway rider. If you've ever used the New York subways, you know their walls are irresistible attractions to graffiti artists of all ages — people who draw pictures and scrawl messages: some obscene, some sad, some hostile, and some prophetic.

But the message I remember best appeared on an advertising poster depicting an austere, dignified, old gentleman recommending a particular product. Someone — perhaps a little boy writing the naughtiest thing he could think of — had sketched a balloon coming out of the man's mouth containing the words, "I like grils."

Underneath, someone had written with a felt-tipped pen, "It's girls, stupid. Not grils."

And below that, in still another handwriting style, someone else had written, "But what about us grils?"

The whimsy and insight of that third message

made me wish I could meet the author, for it re-minded me of the marvelous good news of the Gospel: when we are honest with ourselves and a few others we find that all of us are really "grils" — oddballs and misfits. This is good news for the universal race of those who don't fit in: losers, odd ones, the peculiar, and the out-of-step.

Word for the Day: Luke 5:31-32

> "Jesus answered them, 'It is not the healthy who need a doctor, but the sick. I have not come to call the righteous, but sinners to repentance.'"

Consciousness Raiser and Application

The devil is known as "the father of lies," and there are two lies in particular which destroy life, fellowship, and communication like no others. One is a lie about God: that He does not exist, or if He does exist, that He does not love you, or that there is a limit to His love.

The other lie is one about yourself, and that's the lie we want to think about today. If the devil can make you lie about who and what you are to your-self and to others, he has succeeded in making you non-negotiable as a "fellow citizen(s) with the saints and members of the household of God."

To believe that I am totally unlike anyone else, so much better or so much worse, means that I dare not risk revealing myself. Inevitably this closes any possibility for relationship with others.

Now in point of fact, all of us are "grils" and all of us think of ourselves as grils in some area. But our fear is that we are the only grils in the world. Today your assignment is to look for those things in you that make you feel like a gril. It may be some fear or habit, an ambition or hope, anything about you that makes you feel cut off from other people.

When you have found the thing that makes you feel most like a gril, prayerfully look for someone to whom you can reveal that insight before the day is over. It might be a stranger or it might be your best friend. It might be your spouse or one of your children. It might be your secretary or your employer, a salesman or a customer. But whoever it is, find a way to simply reveal something that makes you feel like a gril.

Certainly there is no guarantee of a 100 percent positive response. However, as we begin to discover that our peculiarities do not necessarily cut us off from people, we may even begin to find the Body of Christ.

The Body of Christ is made up of sinners, not the righteous. When we share our righteousness with one another, our good deeds, our record of church and Sunday school attendance, it does not seem to build relationships. When we share our fears or inadequacies, our gril-like attitudes or behavior, people can respond as one human being to another human being.

30 Days to a New You

Prayer

Oh Lord, make me secure enough in the knowledge that I'm Yours, whatever I may do or be, to risk a very private and secret part of me with another human being. Help me to discover the joy today of squandering myself on another, even if I end up casting my pearls before swine, so that a depth of relationship may begin that would otherwise be impossible. Let me be a part of Your Kingdom-building process this day in one specific relationship.

30 Days to a New You

Journal (my reactions, insights and results)

13

Parable: Stalemate

At a seminar I was leading on broken relationships, a woman turned up who was concerned about
her marriage which she described as a "stalemate."

When pressed for an explanation she said, "My
husband and I never quarrel and are never angry.
We simply have no relationship. He comes home
from work, has dinner, watches television, reads the
paper, and then goes to bed."

"Is it like that every night?" I asked.

"Every night for years," she answered.

"Do you love him?"

"Yes," she said, tears beginning to form in her
eyes, "I love him very much."

"Do you think he loves you?"

"No, I'm sure he doesn't or he wouldn't be so
cold and indifferent."

"Well," I said, "he must love you or he wouldn't
be coming home to this dreadfully boring routine
every night. He would be out doing something a

little more creative or interesting. Perhaps he's hoping that one day something will happen to rekindle the love you shared when you were first married."

"But what can I do?" the woman asked.

"What are you doing now to try to change the relationship?"

"I keep inviting him to our prayer group," she replied, "and I leave books and pamphlets around hoping he will read them."

"Is this working?"

"No," she admitted.

"Then why don't you try something much more radical and costly?"

"Give me a for instance."

I grabbed at something wild. "Some night when he is watching television, why don't you put on your prettiest nightie and your best perfume, jump into his lap and tell him that you love him as much as ever. What do you think his response would be?"

"I'd hate to guess," she giggled.

"But what is the worst thing that could happen?"

Without a moment's hesitation she replied, "He might laugh at me."

"That's true, and this is what faith is all about in the dimension of marriage. To leave tracts and pamphlets around and suggest that your husband come to your prayer group really puts you in a superior and invulnerable position. But to do something like this gives him the chance to respond lovingly or with ridicule. Can you take a risk like that?"

Apparently she decided she would do just that,

for a few days later, back at my office, I got this letter: "Dear Bruce: I did as you suggested and guess what? He didn't laugh!"

Word for the Day: Mark 8:35

> "For whoever wants to save his life will lose it, but whoever loses his life for me and for the gospel will save it."

Consciousness Raiser and Application

I don't have much hope for you or me becoming "good" people in this life. However, I believe with all my heart that you and I can be new beings.

To be radically new by the power of Christ means we can reverse the most deeply ingrained human trait: our self-justifying invulnerability. Everything in me wants to keep you from knowing where I have failed or where I hurt. Rather than admit to being wrong, I will ignore you or put you down or argue my case indefinitely.

To be a new being in Christ means we begin to share in His life. The New Testament speaks of "Christ in you the hope of glory." If He is in us, then we can begin to love with His love which means that we can risk being laughed at, locked out, killed, and even crucified as He was. Our word for the day says you must lose your life to find it. In any relationship, if we try to save our life, justify our stance, our righteousness, our innocence, we shall surely lose it. In today's parable the woman found that her marriage could change at the point where she broke the stalemate and was able to risk being vulnerable with her dearest one.

Your assignment today is to find a way of risking your life in some relationship that means a great deal to you. Instead of suggesting where the other person is wrong, tell him where you are wrong. Instead of implying that he ought to change, tell him where you ought to change. Instead of giving advice, ask for it. In other words, reveal yourself to someone else in such a costly way that he could use your words or deeds against you if he would. As an act of devotion for Christ, be defenseless in the presence of someone you love.

To love is to be vulnerable. May you in your assignment today discover that kind of love and practice it. This will be impossible apart from God's help in Jesus Christ. But being new means that we can change even our most deeply ingrained human tendency.

Prayer
Lord, may I believe You when You say, "Behold, I make all things new." Let me know that by Your indwelling Spirit I can be a new creation. I want to be new most of all in the way I love. I want to love people as You love which means to lay down my life for them. Please help me to so live love that I can be a channel of miracles and healing in relationships.

Journal (my reactions, insights and results)

14

Parable: The Beds

Two dear friends recently moved to our town from Alabama when Sidney retired from his business. His wife, Louise, is a genuine southern belle who has never done a day's work in her life. Raised by maids, she had never made a bed or a cup of instant coffee, let alone clean a toilet. They are now living in a small apartment, and her new task from God is to learn to cook and keep house.

She was making great strides until one dismal morning all the difficulties and frustrations of the past months tumbled in while she was trying to make their two beds.

"Sidney Mohr," she called, "come in here. You see those beds? I am not going to make those beds. What do you think of that?"

Now Sidney is the kind of person I'd like to be — a lover — a Jesus type of guy — and so he understood immediately that the issue wasn't beds at all, and he said gently, "That's all right, dear. We'll sleep in them unmade."

"What do you mean that's all right?" demanded Louise. "You've never slept in an unmade bed in your life and neither have I, and we're not going to start tonight."

"Well," said Sid, "We'll go to a motel."

"What if we come back tomorrow and I still don't feel like making these beds?" asked Louise.

"We'll just stay in the motel until you do feel like making the beds," was Sid's reply.

And suddenly all the rebellion left Louise and she could laugh at the whole infantile struggle against God's present plan for her.

Now that's what a lover does and that's a new kind of love. A lover doesn't respond to the situation or to the agenda at the meeting. A lover says, "Hey, let's get behind that and hear the hurt."

Word for the Day: Mark 5:1-2, 6-7

> "They went across the lake to the region of the Gerasenes. When Jesus got out of the boat, a man with an evil spirit came from the tombs to meet him . . . .
>
> "When he saw Jesus from a distance, he ran and fell on his knees in front of him. He shouted at the top of his voice, 'What do you want with me, Jesus . . . .'"

Consciousness Raiser and Application

In the word for today we hear a mentally sick man

running to Jesus, saying in essence, "Leave me alone!" Jesus responds to his need and intent, not to his words.

Much of our communication with one another is a smoke screen. To say what we really feel or think is far too painful, so we talk around things or alongside of things.

The Gospel gets right to the heart of man's need. If we are to cooperate with God, we must begin to hear people with His ears and to love them with His heart. What people are actually saying has little to do with the words they are using or the issues they are raising.

Today become aware of the people around you and the unspoken things they are saying to you. Try to hear the silent screams or the secret hopes hidden behind their words.

If you have an irritable and careless waitress in the restaurant, instead of commenting on the coffee in your saucer, be aware that something in her recent or distant past has made her hostile. Try to say something to her that will let her know she is a unique child of God of infinite worth and loved by Him.

In the same way, listen to your children, your spouse, your boss, your colleagues, and your neighbors whenever you have an opportunity. Respond with your words and actions to the unspoken thing they are afraid to say and which they are hoping you will hear.

Prayer
Oh Lord, today help me to hear with Your ears the silent pleas and screams that will be hidden behind argumentative and angry words. Help me to respond to confused and aching hearts more than to belligerent and rebellious words.

30 Days to a New You

Journal (my reactions, insights and results)

15

Parable: The Calendar

We probably can tell a lot about ourselves by examining the gifts we give other people. We make jokes about the husband who gave his wife two tickets to the ball game on her birthday, but often the presents we give other people are just as revealing.

I have a calendar in my office which is given to me each year by a friend. It's his business calendar, and at Christmas he sends it to all of his customers. Across the top my calendar says, "This calendar was prepared especially for (in great big print) BRUCE LARSON. And then in very small print it says, "From the E. H. Titchener Company," which is the name of my friend's firm.

This man is trying to act out in his advertising something he profoundly believes. As Christians we are to put the emphasis on the other person, not on ourselves. To be genuinely interested in someone else, to take him and his needs seriously, is more effective than the kind of witness that centers in

30 Days to a New You

"Let me tell you what Jesus has done for me (or worse, through me)."

When God spoke to Samuel in the Temple, He called him by name, "Samuel." He did not say, "This is God." To be in God's presence means we hear Him speak our name. The people we witness to need to feel we know their names, who they are, and where they hurt.

Word for the Day: John 4:28-30

> "Then, leaving her water jar, the woman went back to the town and said to the people, 'Come, see a man who told me everything I ever did. Could this be the Christ?' They came out of the town and made their way toward him."

Consciousness Raiser and Application

The Samaritan woman by the well was so impressed with Jesus that she brought the whole town to see Him. She did not accomplish this by reporting the theological discussion she had had with Him. The townspeople came because of her claim that "He told me everything I ever did."

Carefully examine each conversation you have today. Try to be aware of those things you say or do not say and the effect produced in the listener or listeners. Be especially aware of those things you tend to say to give you status with the other person. With God's help try to produce just the opposite effect today. Prayerfully ask God to help you build other people up. Ask Him to create the impression in your listener or listeners that they are important and that you respect them and love them. There are no rules for this, and your strategy must change with each person you encounter. But God will give you a strategy for each person if you ask Him.

Today the mark of the fact that God lives in you will be measured by how well the people you meet think of themselves after they have been in your presence. Did they feel that you knew their name, that you loved them, and that they were important? If so, they will sense God's Presence.

Prayer
Oh Lord, help me today to put the other person's name in larger type than my own; to relate and listen and interact with another person so that he may come to know something of his own importance to You.

Journal (my reactions, insights and results)

16

Parable: Crazy Charlie

I would love to think of myself as a "St. Francis" type. He is one of my heroes, and though I don't think I have his temperament, I do emulate him every morning when I scatter seed for the birds on our back deck. (My wife has been threatening to buy me a pair of sandals and a brown bathrobe with a hood.)

The example of St. Francis prompted an incident last spring that has given me a better understanding of what it means to communicate the Gospel. One morning as I rode to work on my little motorcycle I almost ran over a big box turtle. Thinking of my hero, I stopped to move him off the road and possibly save his life. But in the midst of my good deed for the day I changed my mind and decided instead to play a trick on him. I put him in my pocket and took him to the office.

All day long that turtle was the center of attention. Beautiful secretaries, busy executives, and assorted

30 Days to a New You

visitors all fussed over him. He sat in air-conditioned splendor eating bacon, bread, peanut butter, lettuce, and whatever his little heart desired. The staff eats lunch together at the office, and on this particular day a friend joined us and brought her guitar. So along with everything else, the turtle heard beautiful music, great singing, and all the while continued to stuff his little belly full of exotic foods.

That night at 5:00 I took him back to the same place in the road where I had found him. I carried him to the side and headed him toward the swamp. And then it hit me! I wondered what kind of a tale he would tell his friends. How could he communicate to them the wonders of air-conditioning, the topography and geography of an office building, the experience of being surrounded by beautiful girls and eating strange foods and hearing wonderful music and singing. I'm sure that from that time forward he became known as "Crazy Charlie" to all the other turtles in the swamp.

There is no way that the authentic experience he had can ever be communicated to his friends. The more he tries, the more alienated and estranged he will become. Crazy Charlie is like so many Christians who have had a dramatic conversion or a mountain-top experience of ecstacy or spiritual heights. They try to relate that experience to people who have no equipment for understanding it, and often they simply alienate others and minimize their own credibility.

Word for the Day: 1 Corinthians 14:16-17

> "If you are praising God with your spirit, how can one who finds himself among those who do not understand say "Amen" to your thanksgiving, since he does not know what you are saying? You may be giving thanks well enough, but the other man is not edified."

Consciousness Raiser and Application

To discover that there is a God who loves us, who cares about us, who forgives us, who has a place in the heavens prepared for us for all time is the most exhilarating experience any human being can possibly have.

It is sad when we let that experience alienate us from those about us. Our witness may be a well-intentioned effort at communicating to our family or friends the wonders of the daily discovery that we are loved and forgiven and belong to the family of God. But we must be aware of what this sounds like to those who have not yet discovered this truth. It sounds as though we are making ourselves equal with God and putting them down as mere humans and unspiritual. Now this is not our intention any more than it might have been Crazy Charlie's intention. Crazy Charlie simply told that which he knew to be true. But how in the world could his brother turtles believe such a story?

No one appreciated God's gift of ecstatic experiences more than Paul. He even writes that he was "in seventh heaven." But this was never the thrust of his message or his method of communication.

Today try to find ways that your own experience of God can help you to step down and identify with your brothers wherever they are. Find ways of saying to people around you, "I am just like you. I hurt. I fear. I am lonely. I doubt. I resent. I am lustful." Now don't do this unless it is true. This is not a gimmick. But the people of God are just like other people, and we can communicate at the point of our common humanity. Jesus left His privileged place in heaven and became one of us, lived with us, and identified with us. To communicate God's love today, identify with the people around you — with their hurts, their problems, their joys, and their hopes — and see what happens.

Prayer
Oh Lord, You know how excited I am about some of the things You have shown me in the recent past. But I pray today You will help me delight in someone else's discoveries, present or potential, about their world and their relationship to You.

Journal (my reactions, insights and results)

Parable: The Church Board

Christians used to speak of "preferring one another in love," and though the phrase has somewhat
gone out of fashion, it's still a principle that might
be applied to all church sessions, boards, and gov-
erning bodies if they are ever to reach what the
Quakers call "a sense of the meeting."

One church session I know of has an interesting
rule. If any kind of proposal is made by a member,
no one can speak against that proposal until he has
first of all said three good things about it. Think of
the affirmation you would get in that framework. If
one elder said, "I think we should tear this church
down and build a new one across the street," you
would have to say things like, "Well, that's an original
idea; the building is certainly old and the plumbing
needs improvement," before you could say, "Listen,
that's the dumbest idea I've ever heard. And besides,
my father built this church."

The ideas being discussed at any meeting are

always secondary to the people sitting in the meeting and their emotional needs. We can practice this in our family situation as well. If your son says he is packing up to go off to Uruguay to harvest grasshoppers, try saying something positive like, "I've always liked grasshoppers." Later you can ask, "Who's going to pay for it?" Whatever the idea, honor the person.

Word for the Day: John 3:17

> "For God did not send his Son into the world to condemn the world, but to save the world through him."

Consciousness Raiser and Application

As Christians, we believe God has come to affirm us in Jesus Christ, not to condemn us. But in our daily life we often communicate condemnation for others by stomping on their dumb, immature, impractical, or irrelevant ideas. And when we criticize their ideas, most people feel *they* are being criticized or rejected.

The application for today is simply to make the rule adopted by the church session I have mentioned a rule for your life. Whether you are at the dinner table, at a meeting, or talking with a friend, before you criticize anyone's idea say something good about it first. This is a way of affirming a person and honoring his idea. After you have said at least one good thing, you can go on to point out fallacies or disagreements.

At the end of the day, evaluate what you think happened to the people you were with as well as your own feelings in each situation. See whether this simple rule helped you to be a participant with God in calling forth gifts in another.

Prayer
Oh Lord, today help me earn the right to criticize by saying three good things about someone else's idea or conviction. Seal my lips from criticism until I have paid the price of some appreciative statements.

Journal (my reactions, insights and results)

18

Parable: The Fish

One summer we took a vacation on a quiet and beautiful Canadian lake where the fishing was reportedly excellent. (I find I'm usually fishing somewhere where the fishing was at its best the week or the season before I got there.)

There were six of us in the rustic lakeshore cottage; my wife and I, our three children, and our daughter's friend. Every morning the two boys and I would go out on the lake before breakfast and try to catch a couple of fish. Then one evening my daughter and her friend asked if they could go with me the next day instead of the boys.

I agreed, and morning found the two girls and me out on the lake in our flat-bottomed boat with its antique outboard motor. Our luck was not good. Heading back towards shore, I was sitting in the middle of the boat untangling a line. Christine was steering, and her friend Jean was sitting in the front.

"Gee, Mr. Larson," Jean said, "I'm sorry we

30 Days to a New You

didn't catch a big one to impress the boys with."

No sooner were these words out of her mouth than a fifteen-inch Northern Pike jumped out of the lake, hit me on the side of the face, and fell into the boat, where it flip-flopped wildly at my feet.

As you read this, do you believe it? I've told this story to a great many people, and the skeptics invariably outnumber the believers.

That, of course, was our problem: how to make this good news believable. As we pulled into the dock, the boys were waiting for us. I held up the fish and one of the boys said, "Not bad. How did you catch him?"

You may be sure that we spent most of the morning trying to convince the boys that the fish really had jumped into the boat. As a matter of fact, I'm not sure they ever were convinced.

Word for the Day: Acts 12:12-16

> ". . . he went to the house of Mary the mother of John, also called Mark, where many people had gathered and were praying. Peter knocked at the outer entrance, and a servant girl named Rhoda came to answer the door. When she recognized Peter's voice, she was so overjoyed she ran back without opening it and exclaimed, 'Peter is at the door!'
>
> 'You're out of your mind,' they

told her. When she kept insisting that it was so, they said, 'It must be his angel.'

But Peter kept on knocking, and when they opened the door and saw him, they were astonished."

Consciousness Raiser and Application

Our word for the day reminds us that no one is totally free from the sin of unbelief. Even the apostles in the early church doubted as we do!

When Peter was thrown into prison, his fellow disciples were so worried that they decided to hold an all-night prayer meeting for his safety and release. Meanwhile, an angel of the Lord released Peter from prison and he turned up knocking at their door. When the servant girl reported that the answer to their prayers was standing outside, the disciples said she must be crazy. And when Peter was finally admitted and stood among them, they were still full of unbelief.

Even for believers it is difficult to accept the fact that God can provide all we ask and think. How much more difficult it is for those who do not yet believe to accept the reality and totality of God's love. To tell someone that God loves them unconditionally just as they are is news too good to be true. No one has ever loved them that way. Why should God?

Today you have a double assignment. First, begin to believe the great central truth that you are loved just as you are and that the daily miracles for which you pray can happen. Your prayers can affect the lives of friends, enemies, colleagues, society, and even the world. *Believe* that peace can come. *Believe* that enemies can be reconciled. Ask God for the gift of belief.

But the other assignment for today is to bear witness to your faith in such a way that news too good to be true will be believable to the people who hear. Be patient with their unbelief. Understand that no one is ever totally free from the problem of unbelief.

Prayer

Lord, the love revealed in Your life and death and resurrection and present now in Your indwelling Spirit is beyond my human capacity to believe. I can only accept this because You have given me the gift of belief. Help me today to believe that the things for which I pray are not just a possibility but a reality. Help me to expect them. And, Lord, help me also to understand those about me who find belief difficult. Help me to communicate my belief in ways that will encourage them to trust more.

Journal (my reactions, insights and results)

19

Parable: The Conductor

Squeezing into a crowded PATH train at Newark, New Jersey, one cold morning, I was shocked and astonished to hear a warm and friendly voice coming over the loudspeaker system, "Good morning! Welcome to the PATH Railroad! Get ready for a great day in Fun City."

Those who live in the metropolitan New York area or those who have visited it recently will realize how shocking it was to hear a greeting like that on a subway train.

I cannot remember all that the conductor said, but he was truly a pastor to a worried, harried, hurried bunch of commuters rushing into Manhattan. He had a friendly greeting at each stop, and as people left the train he would open his window and call out a personal word to various ones whom he had come to know during his tour of duty on that line.

When I got off, I could not resist going over and talking to him. He told me that several years before

God had brought about a real change in his life which had altered his whole life style. This man was caring for people as he daily conducted commuters into New York City. I wondered how many people had spoken to that conductor as I did, commenting on his friendly attitude and giving him the opportunity to bear witness to the source and motivation of his life style.

Word for the Day: John 2:7-11

"Jesus said to the servants, 'Fill the jars with water'; so they filled them to the brim. Then he told them, 'Now draw some out and take it to the master of the banquet.'

They did so, and the master of the banquet tasted the water that had been turned into wine. He did not realize where it had come from, though the servants who had drawn the water knew. Then he called the bridegroom aside and said, 'Everyone brings out the choice wine first and then the cheaper wine after the guests have had too much to drink; but you have saved the best till now.'

This, the first of his miraculous signs, Jesus performed in Cana of

Galilee. He thus revealed his glory,
and his disciples put their faith
in him."

Consciousness Raiser and Application

It's difficult to believe that the first recorded public
miracle of our Lord was one that seems so frivolous.
There was a wedding feast and the wine was all gone.
The bridegroom would be embarrassed because he
had not provided sufficiently for his guests. Sensing
this, Jesus turned ordinary water into wine so that the
party might go on and the bridegroom might be
spared any humiliation.

There certainly doesn't seem to be anything
"spiritual" in this incident. And it does seem that
Jesus might have chosen a more dramatic way of
revealing His power and identity. But the strange
thing is that seeing this miracle, His disciples put
their faith in Him.

Is it possible that Christ wants you and me to be
those who bring the wine of joy and celebration to
life? Are we, too, called to ease others in their embarrassment and to make life more fun? I suggest
this is not a bad place to begin. This is the motive
for the first recorded miracle of our Lord, and He
has commanded us to love one another as He has
loved us.

Your assignment today is to try to bring into some
dreary situation something that will give people
warmth, life, and merriment. Today try to turn the
water of dullness into the wine of celebration, em-

barrassment into joy, for Jesus' sake.

Prayer
Lord, You have commanded me to love my brothers and sisters as You have loved me. I'm reminded anew that You were never too busy or too important to bring joy to a wedding party or to alleviate the embarrassment of a friend. Help me today to be a person who can bring joy to a routine experience and fun to a humdrum job, and may I have a spirit of graciousness that puts others at ease in each situation.

Journal (my reactions, insights and results)

Parable: The Escalator

At 5:00 on a winter Wednesday I entered New York's Port Authority bus terminal. I was hurrying home for a quick dinner and then on to conduct a mid-week service at a nearby church. The usual crowd was lined up behind the escalators that take suburban passengers to their buses. Briefcase in one hand and newspaper in the other, I got in line and began the commuter shuffle.

Just as I got to the head of the line, a hard-faced, middle-aged woman came up from the side, shoved in front of me, planted her elbow in my stomach, and stepped onto the escalator.

Now I maintain that there is nothing easy about the Christian life, and every year I see more clearly the complications of radical obedience. What should I say to such a person? I know what I would have said a few years ago — but I am no longer free to put someone like that "in her place." I know what I would like to say. I would like to be a St. Francis kind of Christian who genuinely loves birds and flowers and little children with sticky lollipops and even pushy unlovely people in bus terminals.

Being somewhere between my former condition and my ideal one, I removed the woman's elbow from my stomach and said with elaborate sarcasm, "Forgive me. I didn't mean to shove you."

Her reaction was devastating. She turned and, since she was only a step or two ahead, looked me straight in the eye. Her face seemed to fall apart — all her wrinkles changed position. "I don't understand it," she said with apology and shock. "Why are you so nice to me? I was really rude. I shouldn't have shoved in line like that."

I was at a loss for words. The woman had reacted to my counterfeit display of love as if it were real, and for the moment at least she was transformed. I began to envision this woman as a person who had been fighting all her life for a place in line. Perhaps she had come from a large family where she had been forced to fight for food and favors and affection. Possibly she had been mediocre in studies or social graces and had to fight her way in school. Even now in some office she might be fighting for promotions or benefits or a preferred place on the vacation list. Perhaps this was the first time someone with whom she was fighting for a place in line seemed to be giving it to her graciously.

At this point, I gathered my wits enough to mumble something like, "It doesn't hurt to be nice to people." Then I ran headlong for my bus.

Headed for New Jersey, I sat in bewildered embarrassment. I had seen myself clearly. "Lord," I prayed silently, "how can I preach tonight? What are You trying to teach me?"

Finally He seemed to say, "Bruce, I've been trying to tell you and all My people for centuries that life on this earth will not be changed by preaching and teaching and committees, but by people giving up their rightful place in line — every kind of line — simply because I gave up My rightful place when I came to earth to be among you. What I ask is that you who profess to believe in Me do the same."

I never step on an escalator now without looking about wistfully for someone to slam in ahead of me — but no one does. Jesus has something radically different in mind for me: He wants me to give up my rightful place in my home, office, professional circle, church, and neighborhood. If I can just remember my Lord's strategy, I may see miracles.

Word for the Day: Philippians 2:3-7

> "Do nothing out of selfish ambition or vain conceit, but in humility consider others better than yourselves. Each of you should look not only to your own interests, but also to the interests of others. Your attitude should be the same as that of Christ Jesus: Who, being in very nature God, did not consider equality with God something

to be grasped, but made himself nothing, taking the very nature of a servant, being made in human likeness."

Consciousness Raiser and Application

Jesus says, "Greater love hath no man than this that a man lay down his life for his friends." Now I suppose I have always interpreted this to mean that I should do kind and caring and necessary things for needy people. I suppose I even considered that at some point in my life I might be asked to literally die for my belief in Jesus. In imagining situations where this might occur, I had no doubt that I would be shot gladly for my Lord.

In our word for the day we discover that Jesus, being equal with God, came down from the eternal heavens and became one of us and gave Himself to the world. This is what servanthood is all about. He came among us as one of us to meet our needs. When He became an offense to us, we killed Him. And He submitted to this.

Now the difficult thing He is asking is that we do the same for others. He asks us to leave our exalted position as those who have better jobs, more knowledge, more faith, more money or more of anything that the world deems important, to come among those who have less and be at their disposal. Our word for the day means simply that we give up our rightful place in line to those who are undeserving.

To be more specific, I am suggesting that today

you examine the areas where people are contesting with you for a place not rightfully theirs: in your office, factory, school, home, or neighborhood. This is where you can exhibit true Christian faith and give up your rightful place. If you do this simply to avoid conflict, it doesn't count! But if, from a position of strength, you choose not to fight for your rights, for Jesus' sake, you are doing the very thing He commanded us to do.

So today look for the places where undeserving people are trying to put you down: on escalators, in subways and buses, in committees, on office staffs, and in schools. To give them the place which is rightfully yours is a silent but powerful witness to the fact that this is how you have been loved. It may change the other person or it may not. That is not important. The important thing is that this is our Lord's strategy, and we belong to Him.

Prayer
Lord, help me today to know that You gave up Your rightful place in heaven to come and live with me in my world. Help me to give up my rightful place to other people as freely as You gave up Your place for me.

Journal (my reactions, insights and results)

21

Parable: The Grits

When I joined the infantry during World War II, it was the beginning of many new learning experiences for me. As a seventeen-year-old kid from Chicago, I was sent first of all to Fort Benning, Georgia, for training. My first morning I sat down to breakfast with ten other men at a family-style table. In the center of that table was a large bowl of something that looked like Cream of Wheat. As I scooped up a large amount in my bowl and poured on milk and sugar, I noticed a tall mountain boy across the table staring at me bug-eyed. "Is that the way you eat grits?" he asked.

Now as a Chicago boy I had heard of grits but had never seen them before, and I mentally filed this new information away for future reference. But rather than exhibit my ignorance, I smiled confidently and said, "Oh, yes. This is how we eat grits in Chicago." He watched me in amazement as I finished the terrible tasting concoction. And by keeping my eye on him I discovered that the proper way to eat grits is with butter and salt.

Many mornings later I found myself sitting at the breakfast table with this same rangy mountaineer. Grits were served again, and under his watchful eye I took a bowl, scooped up some grits, and poured on milk and sugar. Somehow I managed to eat the mess. The alternative, which would be to admit my ignorance or error, was unthinkable.

Word for the Day: John 5:2-7

> "Now there is in Jerusalem near the Sheep Gate a pool, which in Aramaic is called Bethesda and which is surrounded by five covered colonnades. Here a great number of disabled people used to lie — the blind, the lame, the paralyzed. One who was there had been an invalid for thirty-eight years. When Jesus saw him lying there and learned that he had been in this condition for a long time, he asked him, 'Do you want to get well?'

> "'Sir,' the invalid replied, 'I have no one to help me into the pool when the water is stirred. While I am trying to get in, someone else goes down ahead of me.'"

Consciousness Raiser and Application

Someone once said that the Gospel is all too often the answer to an unasked question. Certainly the central message of the Gospel is that God offers love, forgiveness, and healing to all those who admit they are in trouble.

But as the story of the grits would indicate, I have great difficulty in admitting I am in trouble or wrong. I'm very much like the man by the pool of Bethesda. He had been ill for thirty-eight years and lay by the pool hoping for a healing. When Jesus came by and asked him if he wanted to be healed, his first response was to blame someone else for his condition. He complained that he had no one to help him into the pool at the right time.

Today your assignment is to learn how to ask for help. Now to ask for help from either God or man is humbling. But I would suggest that if we cannot ask for help from our fellowmen, we probably cannot ask for help from God. The problem lies in our unwillingness to confess our need.

Today open yourself to all that God may want to give you, through His own mysterious transcendence or through the mediation of some other person (believer or otherwise). Practice asking for help. Try to find ways of saying genuinely, "I don't know, please tell me," or "How do you do that?" or "Would you show me . . .?"

As difficult as it is to admit our inadequacies, it is even more difficult to admit we have been wrong. Today may God show you those areas where you have been wrong and enable you to say, "Please forgive me."

But whether our need is for forgiveness or for specific help in some area, it is a beautiful thing to be in the place where we are open to receive from God or from any of His servants.

Prayer

Lord, today make me aware of the number of ways in which You might want to burst into my life through people or through Your own Holy Spirit. Help me to discover my own limitedness and finiteness, my insensitivity and stupidity. Make me someone who can delight in receiving that You might be glorified.

Journal (my reactions, insights and results)

Parable: The Ticket Seller

The Celebration of Evangelism held in Cincinnati was called "A Revolution of Love," and that's just what it turned out to be. It was a unique climate where young and old, black and white, liberal and conservative began to listen to one another, to understand one another, and to love one another.

When we left the celebration on Friday afternoon, I was sure the spirit of love and brotherhood I had found there would last forever. It lasted till I got to the airport and found my flight to Baltimore was overbooked and my confirmed ticket would not be honored. Eight of us who had been at the celebration watched in amazement as the plane took off leaving us behind. Even worse, the airline personnel didn't seem to care.

As we began to voice our anger, it suddenly hit us. If our faith in Jesus Christ which we had been celebrating that week was real, it had to be lived out right there.

With my sense of peace and joy somewhat restored, I began to move to the other airline counters. At one of them I found a young man who immediately said, "Let me see what I can do for you." Getting out his big book, he began figuring and typing on his teletype. "There is a chance you might get on a plane leaving right now for Pittsburgh," he explained, "with a possible connection to Baltimore." I grabbed the ticket he wrote for me and ran to the gate, only to find that plane was also filled!

Crestfallen, I returned to my "chaplain" behind the ticket counter and told him my story. "Don't worry," he reassured me. "We'll find some way to get you there." And he began to check his book again.

Just then a "celebration friend" came up, and I poured out my troubles. "Don," I said, "my faith was being sorely tested by the indifference of that airline down the way, but then I met this man here. He and his company aren't even responsible for my problem, but he's trying to help and has spent all kinds of time on me. Just to know there is someone who cares makes all the difference.

As the two of us talked, the ticket agent looked up and, without saying a word, reached into his inside coat pocket and pulled out a picture of Jesus. Smiling, he held it before us for a moment and then silently put it back again and returned to the teletype and the business of reservations. Speechless for a moment, Don finally said, "Hey, he's one of us, isn't he?" At that point our new friend smiled and handed

30 Days to a New You   **125**

me my ticket for confirmed space on a later flight. "Good luck and God bless," he said.

Now a five-hour delay in getting home is no fun, but meeting that unknown disciple behind the ticket counter made it all worthwhile.

Word for the Day: Acts 16:14-15

> "One of those listening was a woman named Lydia, a dealer in purple cloth from the city of Thyatira, who was a worshiper of God. The Lord opened her heart to respond to Paul's message. When she and the members of her household were baptized, she invited us to her home. 'If you consider me a believer in the Lord,' she said, 'come and stay at my house.' And she persuaded us."

Consciousness Raiser and Application

For many of us it is difficult to think of the market-place as a holy place. We expect to have God touch us and bless us and comfort us in those accustomed institutions we identify with worship or religion or spirituality.

What we forget is that the marketplace is where God's people live most of their lives. After they leave the places of worship, the only place to serve God and their fellow-man is in the marketplace. Elton Trueblood tells a wonderful story about a stranger who came to a Quaker meeting. He was unaccustomed to the silence and embarrassed by it. Finally he turned to someone nearby and said, "When does the service begin?" The man leaned over and replied in a whisper, "The service begins when the worship ends!"

Today you have two assignments. As you head for the marketplace (be it a school, office, factory, or hospital), look for someone along the way to whom you can be a Lydia. Look for someone who needs comfort, money, encouragement, a room for the night, help with some task, or perhaps just a hand with a suitcase or some bundles. As a part of your love for God and therefore for His people, try to be an answer in a specific way to someone else in their need.

The second part of your assignment is to look for someone like Lydia when life becomes oppressive, difficult, confusing, or frightening. Don't retreat into yourself or rush for some familiar place of prayer. Expect God to break into your life through a Lydia — God's person there in the marketplace. Expect someone to say, "May I help you?" Let God surprise you with the unlikely people He might spread about your life today to remind you that you are a part of the family and that you are loved and cared for.

Prayer

Lord, today let me be a Lydia in the marketplace. Let me be someone who can look for another in trouble and offer relevant, specific help. Let me also believe that I am surrounded by Lydias in all kinds of unexpected places. Allow me to receive help from one of Your Lydias this day and give You the praise and the thanks.

Journal (my reactions, insights and results)

23

Parable: The Honda

After twelve years of life as a commuter from a town in New Jersey to New York City, it was a pleasant change to move to Columbia, Maryland, where much of the pastoral countryside of the last century remains unchanged. There are no subways yet! I still miss New York in many ways, but life in Columbia has made it possible to realize one of the dreams of my life — to own a motorcycle.

My fifteen-year-old son was as thrilled about this prospect as I was, and together we shopped around for the right machine. We finally settled on the smallest full-size motorcycle that Honda makes, a Trail 90. This meant my son could use the motorcycle to ride in the woods around our house, and certainly it would be the most economical and adventurous way for me to travel the five miles to and from the office.

Well, it's no small matter getting a motorcycle licensed and registered, not to mention passing the road test. But the great day finally came, and I was ready for my maiden run to the office. Wearing my best business suit and tie and with my briefcase strapped on behind, I ventured forth.

Since about one-fourth mile of the journey entailed traveling on a four-lane super highway, I picked a late morning hour so that I would not get into any heavy traffic. All went well, and by the time I reached the highway I was moving along at a speedy thirty-five miles per hour. Suddenly, coming at me in the opposite direction at about seventy miles per hour was what cyclists refer to as the "ultimate machine." It was a huge Honda 750 carrying a burly young cyclist with his chick hanging on behind, both in black leather jackets, long hair flying out from under each helmet.

As we were about to pass each other, the driver raised his left arm in the "ride on" salute that motorcyclists give. I cautiously looked around to see who was following me and discovered that mine was the only vehicle on the road. Obviously he meant me. I had been accepted into that great fellowship of "easy riders" my first time out! Timidly I gave him back a salute as he whisked by. I could not believe that getting into this mysterious fraternity would be so easy. Simply by spending several hundred dollars for a tiny machine, with no credentials, no experience, and not even the proper uniform, I was one of them — no questions asked!

I rode home from the office that night looking for cyclists. I spotted one a great way off, and before he could even see me clearly, I greeted him with a "ride on" sign which he loyally returned. Since then whenever I ride I find our special fellowship quick to greet one another.

Now to understand what this means to me you have to understand one of the basic anxieties of my life. I have a deep-seated fear of being the odd man out. The one who doesn't fit. The one who is inappropriate for the occasion. I have recurring nightmares of being at a party without my trousers or in the pulpit without a single note or taking an exam for which I have not studied. If the Gospel is to be good news for people like me it has to say, "Welcome. You're one of us. You're home free. Come on in; you belong."

Because of my little motorcycle this is exactly what happened and keeps happening. An exciting group of people have found me acceptable and have included me. And this is exactly the kind of message the church must communicate to the world and to the non-Christian. When someone comes into our worship service, we must somehow non-verbally say to them, "Welcome. You're home. You belong. We're with you."

Word for the Day: John 8:10-11

> "Jesus straightened up and asked her, 'Woman, where are they? Has no one condemned you?' 'No one, sir,' she said. 'Then neither do I condemn you,' Jesus

declared. 'Go now and leave your
life of sin.'"

Consciousness Raiser and Application

One of the sad things about life on this globe is
that so many people are trying to put other people
down. Some of my most painful memories come
from my own childhood experiences or from watching children minimize, humiliate, and shame one
another. Anyone who is different, deformed, unlovely, or awkward has no shortage of people to
point that out to him.

As we get older it seems we are still quick to point
out one another's failings. We may not be as overtly
cruel, but we are quick to make those around us feel
stupid or inferior. Life is so full of situations that
bring out the worst in us. When it rains we say, "Why
didn't you close the car windows?" When we are
behind in our bills we say, "Didn't you mail those
letters?" When we're presented with a low report
card we say, "Didn't you promise me you would
work harder this semester?" When our secretary
misspells a word we say, "Don't you have a dictio-
nary?" When our child spills a glass of milk we say,
"Do you have to be so clumsy?" The list goes on
and on as we are put down or put others down daily
for real or imagined shortcomings.

I am convinced that Jesus came to reverse this
process. When the woman taken in adultery was
brought before Him, there was a whole circle of
fellow human beings condemning and criticizing,

ready to stone her to death — which was, in those days, within their legal rights. Now there was no question about her guilt or the legal punishment of that time. However, our Lord changed the whole emphasis when He said, "Let the innocent one, that is the one who has no error in his life, cast the first stone." When the crowd left, He said to her, "Neither do I condemn you."

Today look for as many ways as possible to say in twentieth century language — to the people at your breakfast table, in your office, in your school, or in your neighborhood — "I believe in you. I do not condemn you. What you did is okay. I understand."

Each time you feel anger rising at someone who has failed you or has hurt another, try to reverse the feeling and say an affirming word to that person about your belief in them. Convey the fact that your acceptance of them does not depend on their performance. Mistakes or failures can be corrected, and it's going to be O.K.

Prayer

Oh Lord, help me to know that the heart of the good news is the fact that we are no longer strangers, but belong to You and to Your Kingdom and to one another. Help me in some tangible way to communicate to another traveler on the road of life that I recognize him as belonging to You and that he is thereby my brother and companion.

Journal (my reactions, insights and results)

PART III

DOING THE WILL OF GOD

God is not only your father or the head of your new family; He also is engaged in radically changing the world and the way men live together in it. The new you needs to be aware of the romance of doing the will of God.

Parable: The Broken Door

When the beds at our house are full and we have to put guests up at our local motel, they never fail to be impressed with it. It's so posh there are even phones in the bathrooms. One evening recently I went there to pick up some friends for a dinner date at our house. As I came into the lobby I felt something sharp on the door, and when I picked up the house phone to announce my arrival I realized blood was running off my thumb, down my arm, and splashing on the counter. Something on the door had removed a whole chunk of skin.

I quickly hung up and rushed over to the reception desk. "Can you girls help me?" I asked. "I've cut my thumb on your door, and I'm bleeding all over your lobby." In no time those two lovely girls produced Kleenex and Band-Aids and had me all fixed up. I was greatly impressed with their speed and efficiency and said so. "Well, actually," said one girl, "you're the third person today to cut his hand on that same door."

I've been wondering since then if that's what happens in my life. Have I gotten so adept at putting on Band-Aids that I never think about how I could prevent the hurts?

Word for the Day: Leviticus 25:9-10, (New English Bible)

". . . and so you shall hallow the fiftieth year and proclaim liberation in the land for all its inhabitants. You shall make this your year of jubilee."

Consciousness Raiser and Application

Most of us enjoy helping other people. It is satisfying to be able to give money or counsel or some particular service to someone else.

The Bible is clear in stating that God does command us always to give the cup of cold water, to share our coat with another, to visit those who are sick or imprisoned. But our word for the day suggests that God also is concerned with the cause of injustice or oppression or evil. The old Jews celebrated the Year of Jubilee, a year in which all debts were canceled, slaves were set free, and land was returned to original owners. As a result of this practice, every fifty years the system was radically altered and a new beginning was made possible.

Today look for the place in your family, your job, your school, or your neighborhood where you can begin to change a destructive pattern. Begin to be aware of those things that hurt and oppress the people around you and try to find the place where you can make a difference. Often people who try to change systems are misunderstood, and we must be prepared for that. But this is our call, and it is as definite as our call to individual charity and good works. We are called to bring about that Year of Jubilee to those who are being exploited, oppressed, dehumanized, or ignored. Today, look for the place where your influence can make a difference.

Prayer
Oh Lord, You know how much I enjoy putting Band-Aids on people's bloody wounds, but today help me to find that which is hurting many and to quietly repair some procedure, rule, law, or way of doing business that will keep people from being hurt.

Journal (my reactions, insights and results)

Parable: The Cab Driver

It was a beautiful fall day in Indianapolis when I stepped off the plane and climbed into a taxi. As we were driving along, I remarked to the driver, "It's really a gorgeous day out here in Indiana."

"You should have been here yesterday," was his response. "It was terrible."

We drove a bit further and I said, "You know, most of our autumn leaves are gone in Maryland, but your trees are still beautiful. I'm glad I came this week."

"These leaves will be gone in three or four days," he predicted.

We came alongside the Indianapolis Speedway where the great car-racing event occurs every Memorial Day.

"Isn't this the Indianapolis Speedway?" I asked.

"Yes," he replied.

"I'd sure like to see the race here some Memorial Day," I said.

30 Days to a New You   143

"I wouldn't go near it," responded the cabby. "I'd rather watch the horses run."

"Ah, you go to the track?"

"No, I never go. It's too expensive."

When we parted, I was struck by the hopelessness of this man's outlook. Even the good days are bad because they will soon change. My cab driver's motto seemed to be, "Behind every silver lining there is a dark cloud."

By way of contrast, a friend recently sent me a postcard (apropos of nothing) with the following message in his great bold scrawl: "Thought for the day. If you plan to swallow a frog, it is best not to look at it too long. If you have a number of frogs to swallow, swallow the big one first." Signed, "George." The sender is George McCausland, known all over the Pittsburgh area as "Uncle George." He is in demand as a conference speaker, counselor, and encourager of the discouraged.

For "Uncle George" every day is an adventure, and for those who have the privilege of being his friends, that adventure is contagious. You never know when a visit or a phone call or a postcard like the one I received will burst into your day and lift your sights.

Word for the Day: Acts 27:20-22; 33-36

> "When neither sun nor stars appeared for many days and the storm continued raging, we finally gave up all hope of being saved.

30 Days to a New You

After the men had gone a long time without food, Paul stood up before them and said: 'Men, you should have taken my advice not to sail from Crete; then you would have spared yourselves this damage and loss. But now I urge you to keep up your courage, because not one of you will be lost; only the ship will be destroyed . . . .

"Just before dawn Paul urged them all to eat. 'For the last fourteen days,' he said, 'you have been in constant suspense and have gone without food — you haven't eaten anything. Now I urge you to take some food. You need it to survive. Not one of you will lose a single hair from his head.' After he said this, he took some bread and gave thanks to God in front of them all. Then he broke it and began to eat. They were all encouraged and ate some food themselves."

Consciousness Raiser and Application

The storm had lasted fourteen days. All of the professional sailors were terrified as were the passengers. They had thrown the cargo and much of the rigging overboard. They had even tied ropes around the ship to hold it together in the storm.

People were so terrified that for fourteen days they had neglected eating.

In the midst of all this, a word of assurance came from one little landlubber. He told the professionals on board not to worry — God had told him that not a single person would die. He then urged them to eat, broke bread, gave thanks, sat down, and initiated a picnic in the midst of the storm. Encouraged, they all joined him.

Hope is contagious! Hope is the thing that sustains one person through an ordeal of unbelievable hardship, a prison camp or death march, while others perish.

Hope is a gift of God. You cannot generate hope by self-effort any more than you can generate faith or love. It is God's to give and ours to receive if we want it.

Perhaps the most remarkable quality of hope is its contagiousness. Jesus spoke about His followers being leaven or salt. Our word for the day demonstrates that one person with hope can change the attitude on a sinking ship. One person with hope can change an office. One person with hope can make a classroom more bearable or more fun.

Today, ask for the gift of hope and then begin to exercise it wherever you are sent. It may be that in the midst of some tense meeting you'll be able to simply say, like Paul, "Let's take a break and have something to eat." Receive the gift of hope today and share it with your family, friends, and colleagues in a specific way.

Prayer
Lord, I know that You live in me when people around me are encouraged; when they can take themselves and their problems less seriously because I am there. Help me to find ways today to celebrate life in every encounter, even those over the telephone or by letter. May I become a contagious person sharing hope with others for Your sake.

Journal (my reactions, insights and results)

Parable: E=MC²

When I was a student at Princeton Theological Seminary, I had a very distinguished neighbor. Albert Einstein was at that time teaching at the Institute for Advanced Studies and lived next door to the seminary.

One Sunday when I was returning from church, I saw him out walking. He was wearing his usual sweatshirt and sneakers. His long white hair was flying in the breeze (he was the original hippy), and he carried the Sunday paper. This is my chance, I thought. I rushed up to him and said, "Good morning, Dr. Einstein." He said, "Good morning." Then for three blocks we walked side by side and I couldn't think of a thing to say.

I guess Albert Einstein will always be one of my heroes. I've been told that back in 1904 when scientists were propounding the law of the conservation of matter (matter can't be destroyed, they said, it just changes form), Einstein, who could hardly pass a course in science or math in his early school years, said, "I don't believe that." And, of course, his research finally led to the splitting of the atom where it was discovered that the weight of the two halves was less than the total. Something called energy was released. Out of that came the famous $E=MC^2$ formula that has ushered us into a new age. All because one man believed that the best ideas hadn't been thought of yet.

Well, I believe that God's best ideas about how life can be lived on this tiny spaceship Earth have not yet been discovered. When I was a boy, Tinker Toys were popular, and I was thrilled to receive a box of them one Christmas. The picture on my little $1.98 box showed all kinds of fantastic things that could be built. But my box didn't have enough spools and spindles to produce the wonderful ferris wheel in the picture. I finally realized that I needed box X-23 for $14.00 complete with a motor to make the things I wanted. I was trapped in a limited system — only able to build the few things I had sufficient pieces for.

Do you believe you have all the pieces of God's thinking right now and simply have to figure out a way to make those pieces work? I believe God is aching to give us new insights into what it means to be the incarnation of His love and the tools to implement those insights so that we won't have inadequate spiritual Tinker Toys. I believe that the best ways are still in the mind of God. He is waiting for people who do not think in terms of a closed system

— people like Albert Einstein. And, potentially, you and me!

Word for the Day: Revelation 21:1-4

"Then I saw a new heaven and a new earth, for the first heaven and the first earth had passed away, and there was no longer any sea. I saw the Holy City, the new Jerusalem, coming down out of heaven from God, prepared as a bride beautifully dressed for her husband. And I heard a loud voice from the throne saying, 'Now the dwelling of God is with men, and he will live with them. They will be his people, and God himself will be with them and be their God. He will wipe every tear from their eyes. There will be no more death or mourning or crying or pain, for the old order of things has passed away.'"

Consciousness Raiser and Application

In the Book of Revelation, John was able to visualize that which was invisible and to claim it as a coming reality. He knew that because Jesus Christ came to live among us, things could not and should not be the same. He saw the implications for life on this earth and beyond.

Today, look at life about you in your particular

world: your home, school, neighborhood, or business. Believe that the best way of doing your particular job and of living life in your particular setting has not yet been found. Believe that God is eager to have someone like you discover a new dimension of His liberating, creative will for men in that situation.

You might simply come up with a way to make the job easier or more fun. You might be able to change unjust laws or rules that oppress or dehumanize other people. Believe that God is a creator who is even more eager to give us new blueprints, new guidelines, new methods, and new ways, than we are to ask. Today let God show you your piece of the world through new eyes. Begin to initiate changes, however small, that can make life new and different for those around you.

Prayer
Lord, You are not only the Redeemer of the world, but You are the Creator and the Recreator of the universe. Help me today to see the world through Your eyes. Help me to participate with You in the exciting work of recreation that will bring liberty and joy to many about me.

Journal (my reactions, insights and results)

Parable: English Leather

Early one morning I had to catch a plane from
Newark, New Jersey, to Syracuse, New York, having
returned late the previous night from leading one
conference and on my way to another.

I was tired. I had not budgeted my time wisely,
and I was totally unprepared for the intense schedule
before me. After rising early and hastily eating breakfast, I drove to the airport in a mood that was anything but positive. By the time the plane took off, I
felt so sorry for myself, and so guilty because I was
unprepared, that I hated God and myself and the
people who had invited me to come to lead this
conference.

Sitting on the plane with an open notebook in
my lap, I prayed, "Oh, God, help me. Let me get
something down here that will be useful to Your
people in Syracuse." About halfway through the
brief flight, a stewardess came down the aisle passing
out coffee. The passengers were all men, and as the

stewardess approached my seat I heard her exclaim, "Hey! Someone is wearing English Leather After Shave Lotion. I can't resist a man who uses English Leather. Who is it?"

Eagerly I waved my hand and announced, "It's me!"

The stewardess immediately came over and sniffed my cheek while I sat basking in this sudden attention. All through the remainder of the flight we maintained a cheerful banter each time she passed my seat. Twenty-five minutes later when the plane prepared to land, I realized that my temporary insanity had vanished. Despite the fact that I had failed in every way — in budgeting my time, in preparation, and in attitude — everything had changed. I was freshly aware that I loved God and that He loved me.

What is more, I loved myself and the people around me and the people who were waiting in Syracuse. I was like the Gerasene demoniac after Jesus had touched him — clothed, in my right mind, and seated at the feet of Jesus. I looked down at the notebook in my lap and found a page full of ideas that could prove useful through the weekend.

"God," I mused, "how did this happen?" It was then I realized that someone had entered my life and turned a key. It was just a small key, turned by an unlikely person. But that simple act of affirmation, that undeserved and unexpected attention, had transformed me from someone in a deep depression into a sane, mature Christian.

30 Days to a New You

Word for the Day: Matthew 14:25-31

> "During the fourth watch of the night Jesus went out to them, walking on the lake. When the disciples saw him walking on the lake, they were terrified. 'It's a ghost,' they said, and cried out in fear. But Jesus immediately said to them: 'Take courage! It is I. Don't be afraid.'
>
> 'Lord, if it's you,' Peter replied, 'tell me to come to you on the water.'
>
> 'Come,' he said.
>
> Then Peter got down out of the boat and walked on the water to Jesus. But when he saw the wind, he was afraid and, beginning to sink, cried out, 'Lord, save me!'
>
> Immediately, Jesus reached out his hand and caught him. 'You of little faith,' he said, 'why did you doubt?'"

Consciousness Raiser and Application

Peter was the disciple to whom Jesus said, "You are Peter (rock), and on you I will build My church." Jesus was depending on Peter to establish His Kingdom after His death and resurrection. And yet He also said to Peter, "You of little faith." Well, every believer is at best a man of little faith. But the Bible tells us that a faith the size of a grain of mustard seed will move mountains.

Today your assignment is to look for people who are already believers, fellow apostles and fellow priests in the Kingdom of our Lord, and yet who are those of little faith. Many of those same people, because they have taken their discipleship seriously, have attempted some great task or have launched out on some new adventure but have begun to sink. They have temporarily forgotten that a little bit of faith is sufficient. In a state of fear and spiritual myopia, they have forgotten that Jesus Christ said He was adequate for all situations. Today, look for a sinking brother or sister who is caught up in intro-spection, self-doubt, fear, or any one of a thousand forms of unbelief.

Try to find a way to give that person the word of affirmation or encouragement that will trigger again a belief adequate for their situation. As our Lord stretched out a hand to Peter, perhaps your word today can help someone who is sinking to continue the task entrusted to him.

Prayer
Oh Lord, may I no longer believe that there are some people who do not have problems with faith and obedience. Help me today to be aware that, for the most part, there are only disciples like me — people for whom faith is at best a sometime thing. Help

me to be the one who can say the word that will enable a brother or sister to believe in his or her own worth once again and in Your love and power.

Journal (my reactions, insights and results)

Parable: Six Priests

Several years ago while leading a conference in Bloomington, Illinois, I suddenly became ill. I had developed all the symptoms that go with flu, including chills and fever. Finally, unable to go on with my responsibilities for leading and speaking, I took to my bed in the men's dormitory.

My sudden illness was announced to those at the conference, and within an hour an amazing parade of people turned up to offer help. The first anointed me with oil for healing — my first experience of this ancient rite of the church. The next one simply wanted to kneel by my bed and offer prayer for me. The third person was a woman doctor who gave concrete medical help. She dosed me with aspirin, took my pulse, and reassured me that in all probability I had a twenty-four-hour flu bug. The fourth person brought me a tray of food which was the last thing in the world I wanted at that time. The fifth person just popped in to express concern and love, while the sixth, and last, was a wonderful Finnish masseuse who sang hymns in her native language while she gave me a massage.

Two things happened. First, I was healed within the hour. I don't know which one of those people was the channel of God's healing, but I suspect they all were used. But even more exciting, I became aware that God was teaching me to receive help from Him through others. Now it has always been much easier for me to give than receive, and that has often caused a block in relationships. I still thank God for the lesson He taught me through my six teachers.

Word for the Day: John 6:5,9,10

> "When Jesus looked up and saw a great crowd coming toward him, he said to Philip, 'Where shall we buy bread for these people to eat?' ... 'Here is a boy with five small barley loaves and two small fish, but how far will they go among so many?' ... There was plenty of grass in that place, and the men sat down, about five thousand of them."

Consciousness Raiser and Application

In Jesus' life and ministry there are two constants in His relationships with people. First, Jesus often asked for help. So many encounters that are recorded in the New Testament begin by His request for a drink or food or lodging or for someone to pray with Him.

Secondly and most surprising, Jesus seemed to ask help of the most unlikely people and expected help from such unlikely sources. In our word for the day, a small boy with only a basket lunch becomes a resource for feeding five thousand people.

With Jesus as your model, try these two constants in your relationships today. Be ready to ask for help, and expect that help from some unlikely sources. In the problems you have today, seek answers from people you would not normally include.

For example, as a parent you might ask your children to help you with some problem that affects the home or even something outside the home. You might be surprised at what this can do for your relationship with them. You might even get some answer that the wisest counselor could not have given. For next to the Lord, who knows you better than your children!

If you are the manager of a department or the head of a business, try consulting someone at a lower level of management for a solution to a plant or office problem. Sometimes the person who works at the bottom of the organizational ladder sees more concretely the real bottlenecks or possibilities.

If you are in some academic center, try asking a student there for an answer to a teaching or administrative problem. A young person might get a new perspective on his or her problem from a senior citizen and vice versa.

Try these two things today, then. Learn to ask for help more readily, and allow God's answer to come from hitherto unsuspected channels. In other words, do not limit the means by which your cry for help can be heard. Let God surprise you, not only with the answer, but with His means of revealing that answer.

Prayer

Lord, help me to believe that You love me and that Your love can only come at the place where I am ready to receive. Beyond that let me know that You have an infinitely creative way of revealing Your will in my life. Let me not despise any one of Your creatures, but honor all people as instruments of Your grace, wisdom, caring, and love.

Journal (my reactions, insights and results)

Parable: The Mediator

'Twas the week before Christmas and all through the bus not a creature was stirring. We were packed in like sardines, with even standing room at a premium as regular commuters vied with last-minute shoppers for space. The road was slippery, traffic was heavy, and the bus was behind schedule. An atmosphere of irritation and gloom prevailed that was anything but a "holiday spirit."

I was standing near the center of the bus, facing sideways to catch the bit of light available for reading. In the seat just below me were two men wearing caps and leather jackets. They seemed somewhat out of place among the crowd of white-collar workers. One was a man of middle years, the other a boy of twenty or so. I assumed they were father and son. Just behind them were two nuns, chatting amiably and glancing from time to time at their open missals.

Suddenly the bus lurched to a stop and, caught off balance, I grabbed for a handhold to keep from falling. In doing so, I struck a glancing blow to the head of the older man seated below. It must have felt like a karate chop!

Immediately I began to apologize and express my hope that he wasn't hurt, but he would not be placated. Instead, he denounced my carelessness in abusive language, especially for reading when I should have been holding on. My attempts to interrupt him and repeat my apology only enraged him further.

At this, the woman standing next to me got into the act. Indignant over the man's attitude, she let him know how difficult it was to be a standee.

"I paid for my seat!" he shouted.

"I paid for a seat too!" she promptly replied.

At that he became more angry than ever. I fully expected him to get up and punch me in the nose. The young man with him tried to calm him down to no avail. Suddenly, with supreme sarcasm, another standee said, loud enough for the entire busload to hear: "Merry Christmas, everybody!"

The grim greeting brought an end to the scene which had involved all those in the immediate area. That is, all except the two nuns. They were busily reading their missals, looking neither right nor left.

Much later at the first major stop, many people got off, including my angry "friend." The young man did not leave with his companion, and I sat down beside him. As soon as I was settled, he smiled and said, "I hope you will forgive him for the way he acted. You really picked the worst possible time to tangle with him. He's a bricklayer, and today he had an accident that almost cost him his hand. The foreman has threatened to fire him. Not only that, but he is having trouble with his wife."

"Is he a friend of yours?" I asked.

The boy shook his head. "I never saw him before. I'm a college student home for the holidays. We just happened to sit next to each other, and he told me his story."

It occurred to me that we had lived through an incident typical of what happens in each of our lives many times a day. The setting may be an office, a home, a factory, a school, a board room, a church, or any of the many backdrops against which we live out our lives. The circumstances may be different, but the cast of characters is the same. There are the offenders (the role I played in this case), the offended (the bricklayer), the "sidetakers" (those who by word or attitude defend or attack either of the antagonists), and lastly, the uninvolved (in this case, the two nuns).

But in the midst of this scene there was also a priest, a mediator — the young student who tried to bridge the gap between the bricklayer and me. Speaking separately to the offended one and the offender, he tried to remove the barriers of misunderstanding.

Word for the Day: Matthew 5:9
"Blessed are the peacemakers, for they will be called sons of God."

Consciousness Raiser and Application

One of the great mistakes I make in reading the Bible is to try and spiritualize everything I read. Now while there are some tremendously profound words and events that can only be understood through spiritual discernment, most of the Bible contains clear and specific directions that are simple to understand but not easy to do.

The Beatitudes are a prime example of this. One of the Beatitudes is a simple injunction from Jesus to be peacemakers.

What does it mean to be a peacemaker? Well, the definition is not at all complicated. To begin with, it is the opposite of being a troublemaker. A peacemaker is someone who tries to reconcile two people who are having a disagreement. We can be peacemakers and reconcilers for two individuals or two groups in our home, our church, or our school system. One doesn't have to wait to serve at the United Nations and be engaged in the business of reconciling nations to take Jesus' word literally.

And so today, if you are a follower of Jesus Christ and believe in the priesthood of believers, become aware of people in your life who need reconciliation. Probably each has a good reason for disliking or mistrusting or misunderstanding the other. Your job is to begin to prayerfully and lovingly interpret the actions of each to the other in such a way that peace and understanding may result. Perhaps there is no more difficult task than this one that our Lord has given us so clearly. But the simplicity of it is staggering. With His help, you and I can become peace-makers and priests to one another.

Prayer
Lord, give me the audacity to believe that You would have me stand between two unhappy, disagreeing, anxiety-filled, angry people as Your peacemaker. Give me Your Spirit that I might interpret each to the other in the best light. Let me be one who can bring reconciliation between men because You have reconciled me to God through Your life in me.

Journal (my reactions, insights and results)

Lou -

I THOUGHT THIS DEVOTIONAL MIGHT BE APPROPRIATE FOR TONITE - PLEASE FEEL FREE TO MARK IT HOWEVER YOU WANT TO FOR USING TONITE

TNX

GORDON.

30

Parable: The Bus

For many years I traveled to my New York office by bus. The only positive part of that long tedious trip was that I was often able to use the time to get some necessary work done. One day I was especially eager to work on something pressing, and I took a seat over the wheel, hoping that no one would sit next to me, and spread my briefcase and papers on the adjoining seat.

At the last stop before expressing into New York, the seat beside me was the only one unoccupied. Two people got on the bus: a well-dressed young man and a frail and elderly woman, and the young man beat her to the seat.

For several minutes I sat fiercely resenting this young man next to me. But being a Christian means that God deals with our resentments, and I began to lose mine in my concern and compassion for the woman who was having a difficult time staying afoot as the bus lurched about.

30 Days to a New You   *171*

I began to pray that someone would give her a seat. It was unthinkable that I should give up mine because I had work to do and one cannot work standing up on a bus. Before long, however, the Lord let me know that I was sitting on the answer to my prayer.

Trading my irrelevant prayer for some relevant action, I offered the woman my seat. Then as I stood in the aisle, my focus was once again on the young man sitting just beneath me. In the midst of feeling smug about being both a gentleman and a Christian, I realized what I really needed was a new and right spirit.

Here was a lesson for me in microcosm. In a short space of time I had moved from (1) resentment to (2) concern to (3) irrelevant prayer to (4) relevant action to (5) relevant action with the right spirit.

MIGHT SHOW THE "OPPOSITE" TO STAGES OF A BAD DELIM.

Word for the Day: Acts 10:9-15, 19, 20

". . . Peter went up on the roof to pray. He became hungry and wanted something to eat, and while the meal was being prepared, he fell into a trance. He saw heaven opened and something like a large sheet being let down to earth by its four corners. It contained all kinds of four-footed animals, as well as reptiles of the earth and birds of the air. Then a voice told Peter, 'Get up,

30 Days to a New You

Peter. Kill and eat.'

'Surely not, Lord!' Peter replied. 'I have never eaten anything impure or unclean.'

The voice spoke to him a second time, 'Do not call anything impure that God has made clean.' . . .

While Peter was still thinking about the vision, the Spirit said to him, 'Simon, three men are looking for you. So get up and go downstairs. Do not hesitate to go with them, for I have sent them.'"

Consciousness Raiser and Application

The Bible is the most exciting book in the world to me. Not just because I believe it is the Word of God, but because it is *my* story. All through its pages I keep finding people just like me. If God can work with people like that, love them and use them, then I can take heart and believe that He can love and use me.

Our word for the day comes from the Book of Acts which is an account of the birth and expansion of the Christian church. At this point in the story, Peter had become the acknowledged leader of the early apostles and disciples. All of the believers were looking to Peter for definitive words and actions, for interpretations and new strategies.

Peter's vision occurred while he was visiting in a

home in Joppa where he had just raised a dead girl to life in the name and by the power of Jesus Christ. I am sure Peter was both frightened and humbled at witnessing this miracle, and we are told he returned to the rooftop to pray. In the midst of his prayer a vision came that told him to eat food that no righteous Jew would ever eat.

When a committee came to interrupt his prayers and his spiritual time, the vision had prepared Peter to agree to go with them to the house of a Gentile soldier in Caesarea named Cornelius. What happened there was another miracle. When Peter preached the Gospel to Gentiles for the first time, the Holy Spirit fell on the entire household and new disciples were made.

Today, look for ways that the Holy Spirit might take you from your "spiritual exercises" and give you some specific direction — direction that might seem mundane or trivial or even downright unorthodox or dangerous. Let God interrupt your prayers if He chooses and give you guidance to be obedient in some way.

As you are being interrupted, you may find you have an irritable spirit within you. In this you can certainly identify with Peter and a great number of others since the first century believers. As you set off about your tasks, ask God to put a right spirit within you so that you can be a prepared instrument for doing or being His will in some specific situation. Expect miracles in unexpected places today through your obedience and by God's Spirit.

Prayer

Lord, today I pray that You would deliver me from the temptation of spirituality. Let me know that Your Holy Spirit speaks often in plain, simple, costly, and even repulsive ways. Let me be willing to dirty my hands, to go where I would not choose to go, or to be involved with people whom I have previously despised. Let me be as open to Your new strategy for my life as was Your servant Peter so many years ago.

Journal (my reactions, insights and results)